Wrestling the Angel
Collected Shorter Poems 1947-1977

Wrestling the Angel
Collected Shorter Poems 1947-1977

Robin Skelton

BEACH HOLME PUBLISHING LIMITED
Victoria, B.C.

Copyright © 1994 by Robin Skelton

First Revised Edition, 1994

All rights reserved

First Edition published as *The Collected Shorter Poems 1947-1977* by Sono Nis Press: Victoria, B.C. 1981.

No part of this book may be reproduced or transmitted in any form by any means, electronic or mechanical, including photo-copying, recording or any information storage, retrieval and transmission systems now known or to be invented, without permission in writing from the publisher, except by a reviewer who may quote brief passages in a review.

This edition is published by Beach Holme Publishers, 4252 Commerce Circle, Victoria, B.C., V8Z 4M2 with the assistance of The Canada Council and the B.C. Ministry of Tourism and Culture.

Cover photograph: Stan Funk
Cover Design: Antonia Banyard
Production Editors: Antonia Banyard
                                    Sarah Dodd

Canadian Cataloguing in Publication Data

Skelton, Robin, 1925-
    Wrestling the Angel

    Previous ed. published 1981 under title: The collected shorter poems, 1947-1977
    ISBN 0-88878-350-7

    I. Title:The collected shorter poems, 1947-1977. II. Title.
PS8537.K38A17 1994   C811'.54   C94-091961-0
PR9199.3.S52A17 1994

to the Listeners

Contents

Author's Introductions xv

I Overture 19
Overture

II When I Began 23
The Mark
Responsibility
The Red House
Ancestors
Riches
The Circumcision
The Ladder
The Top
Green Apples
Angel
Long-Distance Runner
Westfield Lane
Long Man's Quarry *
Admission One Shilling *
As I Remember It
The Fishers
Land Without Customs
John Arthur
Letter To An Irish Poet
The Brigg
The Walls
Plums
Apple Loft
Cart Frank
Joe Sampson
Message For My Father

III In Times of War 47
Song of Honour
Big Field
Chapel Hill
The Madras Incident
Remembering Esquimalt
Bread

* Collected here for the first time

vii

VietNam
The Quake
Chakrata
The Window
The Reliquary
Peter
The Memory
Sergeant Casey
War News
Considering Ulysses *
Epilogue *

IV The Undefeated Dead 71
Virginia Road Revisited
Dirty Snow
The Come-back
A Chain of Daisies
An Arrangement of Flowers
City Varieties, Leeds, 1963

V In Cornwall 83
The Ball
West Penwith
Construction and Dialogue
The Slickensides
The Blue Coat
Making
From The Artist's Roof: St Ives 1956
The Cotton Dress
The Night Bride
At The Cavern's Mouth: A Dialogue
The Arrival
Sancreed Churchyard

VI For The Muse 99
The Request
Invocation *
One Word *
The Arrival *
Flamen *
Two Moralities and a Footnote
The Whisper

viii

The Presence
Quaternion
Nine for the Muse

VII Happenings 113
The Happening
Winter Scene
The Shell
Elegy For Dead Splendour
Night Piece
A Ballad of Despair
House and Scholar
Good Time Girl *
Man With Newspaper *
Spilt Coffee *
Public House Dominoes *
A Man Watching *
A Ballad of Johnnie Question
The Street
Guide Book
The Exploration
The Game
Robert Graves, A Snapshot *
An Unfortunate Incident
Two Incidents From the Voyage of the Beagle
Nursery Wallpaper
Discovery
Halcyone
The Net
King and Queen
Coriolanus to Volumnia *
The Birthday *
Statistic *

VIII To Claim Her Love 139
Prothalamion at Midwinter
The Pretence
Nothing of Beauty
Chick *
An Uncertain Meaning
Three Ways of Love
On a Summer Night
She, Unrehearsed

The Hearing
On the Common
The Woman
Cat and Bird

IX Annulets for Eros 153
With Proper Respect *
The End of the Night *
Handfast *
Et Ego in Arcadia *
That Afternoon *
Hubris *
The Setback *
Accursed *
The Journey *
Once More *
Satis Est *
The Primrose *
Young *
Correspondance *

X Bestiary 163
The Birds
Eagle
Moor Hens
Wart Hog
Warning With Emblems
Goat
Lizard
Slug
Scorpion
Lobster
The Cat
Bear
Spider
Toad
Bed Bug
Homo Sapiens

XI In Ireland 181
For Dublin With Love
Swans Sleeping

Song at Twilight
Woodtown Manor, Dublin
First Encounter
Clare Abbey
Suibhne Redivivus
An Irish Album
1. Renaissance
2. The Apple
3. Ditch Logic
4. The Return of Casement
5. Geasa
6. Fallguy of the Western World
Who Weeps for Dedalus
Shem Accompanied
The Return of Suibhne
A Rathmines Evening
At Emmet's Grave
A Saint of the Land

XII The Climbing Wave 207
Today
Aubade
The Hat *
Epistemology *
The Statement
The Gift
Youth & Age
The Secret
By the Lake
Song
Country Song
The Sand in the Oyster
Inconclusive
The Dreamer
Afterwards
On the Moor
The Curious
The Rival
Identity
Suppose
The Separation
The Careful *
The Wakeful One *

Erosion
The Inredulity
The Rejection
The Predicament
Recurrence
Careless Speech
Spell

XIII The Dialect 223
Begging the Dialect
The Word
Ars Poetica
The Fence
Flowers and Jar
The Parking Lot
Answering a Question
Where
The Night Before the Lecture

XIV A New World 231
New Bedford
The Bridge
The Rake
At Walden Pond
Lines for a Lady
Drumbeat
The Inscription
This Friday, Flying Westward
A Slice of lemon
A Poet at Fifty
Poem Ending with a Line by Thomas Kinsella
The Friday Fish
History
A Bad Day Through the Berkshires
Ghost Shirts
One Morning *
Night Poem, Vancouver Island

XV Amores 261
The Forgiveness
The Loyalties
A Dream of Drowning

The Leaf
The Alteration
The Resolution
Duodecorum
Accursed
The Hemispheres
The Evidence
Waiting for a Letter
Aphrodite Pandemos
The Triumph
The Friends
Precipice
The Return
Ashamed
In July

XVI At the Centre 281
At the Centre
Solo
Poem on his Thirty-Fifth Birthday
The Waking
Alison Jane Skelton
A Son Sleeping
Child
The Birth
Undergrowth
The Sparrows
Tenacity
Forty
A Piece of Orange Peel
The Track to the Sea *
On the Eve of All Hallows
The Fortieth Summer
Tiger, Tiger
The Ninth Month
The Beginning
The Anniversary

XVII Travelling Time 305
Tidying the Study
The Caves of Drach (Mallorca)
Rocamadour

Robert Graves in Deya, Mallorca
Three Poems for Two Travellers
At Tutankhamun's Tomb, Thinking of Yeats
The Farewell
The Virgin of Torcello
Lines Upon Viewing the Gilded
Equestrian Statue of King William
the Third at Kingston-Upon-Hull
Entering Firenze
Calanche de Piana (Corsica)
Burning Sticks, Mallorca
Bernardino Luini (Lugano)
Campo dei Fiori
The Traveller *

XVIII Waking and Dreaming 331
The Journal
Three Panels for a Quiet House
The Voices
1. Voice on a Birthday
2. Voice of a Witness
3. Voice from a Confessional
4. Voice of a Finalist
5. Instructions
Dark River
Keep Moving
Dreaming and Waking
Among the Stones
Lakeside Incident
To Someone from Exile
The Doors
Stardust
The Prisoner
The Fell of Dark
The Fool of Time *
The Destination *
The Edge
The Dog in the Night Time
At Lost Lake
The Shore
Across This Distance, In Code, In Plain

Index of First Lines 365
Biography 373

xiv

Author's Preface
for the First Edition

The earliest poem in this book was written in 1947 and the most recent in 1977. The collection as a whole presents what I now wish to be regarded as the canon of my work for that thirty-year period, excluding longer poems, satirical verse, translations, and the productions of the pseudonymous George Zuk. It has been compiled with the invaluable assistance of Charles Lillard, whose judgments have enabled me to clarify my own, and whose editorial acumen is responsible for the organization of the whole. The poems have been taken from the following books and pamphlets as well as from manuscripts: *Patmos and Other Poems* (1955), *Third Day Lucky* (1958), *Begging the Dialect* (1960), *The Dark Window* (1962), *An Irish Gathering* (1964), *Inscriptions* (1967), *Because of This* (1968), *Selected Poems 1947-1967* (1968), *An Irish Album* (1969), *Answers* (1969), *The Hunting Dark* (1971), *Musebook* (1972), *Three for Herself* (1972), *Country Songs* (1973), *Timelight* (1974), *Three Poems* (1977) and *Because of Love* (1977). Several of the poems have not been published previously in book form and some of them appear in print for the first time in these pages.

We have chosen to arrange these poems thematically rather than chronologically. It has been my practice to return over and over again to certain themes and also to particular forms and approaches. Consequently, a chronological arrangement would result in a scattering throughout the book of poems which really belong together. Moreover, I have sometimes taken several years to complete a poem to my satisfaction, and a poem of this kind would appear out of place were it to be given a position dictated by its date of publication. "A Son Sleeping", for example, was first drafted in 1958, but it did not receive its final touches until 1977 and has not been published until now. Other poems, first published here, were not included in earlier books because their attitudes, themes and styles did not sit well with the themes and approaches presented by the collections of the time. In order not to frustrate those readers interested in detecting what progress my work may have made over the years, we have given, in the index of first lines, the dates of first publication of each poem in a book. If a poem has not been published previously, or when the date of publication does not indicate the poem's place in the time scheme at all accurately, we have given, in brackets, the approximate date of the composition of the first complete draft.

The texts of a number of these poems have been revised. I have not, however, permitted revision to alter the tenor of any poem, however much I may now disagree with it. Some dedications which seemed proper at the time of the original publication have been omitted in order to avoid irritating the reader with the notion that there are significances here which he or she may not discover. On the other hand, some dedications have been added. Poems are dedicated to people for several reasons. The first is, quite simply, that the occasion which the poem recalls or celebrates was shared by someone else who, therefore, became a part of the poem's beginnings. The second is that the poem is regarded as being spoken to a particular person, or involves that person in its content. The third, which may include the other two, is that I wish to make a gift to a friend who has, in one way or another, helped or stimulated me towards poetry. In no case does the name of the person to whom a poem is dedicated constitute a part of the poem's message.

I cannot hope to express my thanks here to all those people who have, over the years, helped me to make, improve, and publish my poems. I must, however, mention my earliest teacher, Tom Pay, and my university teachers, and later friends, Wilfred Rowland Childe, G. Wilson Knight, and Bonamy Dobrée. Of my fellow poets who have, at different periods, looked over my work and helped me to improve it, I must name John Montague, Thomas Kinsella, Tony Connor, John Knight, and Carolyn Kizer. Others whose encouragement has meant much to me over the years, and who supported my flagging resolution during times of doubt and depression include Mervyn Strickland, John Gawsworth, Robin MacBean, Alex Currie, John and Barbara Jump, Herbert Read, Kathleen Raine, Jeni Couzyn, Susan Musgrave, John Robert Colombo, J. Michael Yates, Liam Miller, Elizabeth Havelock, Herbert Siebner, William David Thomas, Linda Sandler, Anthony Beale, Carl and Hilda Morris, and Michael and Margaret Seward Snow. To no one am I more indebted, however, than to my wife Sylvia, without whose constant support I do not think the majority of these poems could have been written.

Robin Skelton
Victoria,
British Columbia
1981

Author's Preface
to the Second, Enlarged Edition

In 1989, eight years after the publication of the first edition of this book, a quantity of poems written in the period 1958-1976 and neither published nor considered for inclusion in that collected volume were discovered in the Special Collections division of the University of Victoria Library which houses my archives. They had been deposited there some years earlier and left undisturbed until Ann MacLean, a professional archivist, began to catalogue my papers and asked me to help her date the manuscripts and typescripts. I was surprised at what she had found, and felt that I had, unwittingly, somewhat falsified the record by not including a number of these poems in my Collected Shorter Poems.

These poems were not left out of the individual collections of this period because they were below quality, but for reasons of space. My collection of 1960, *Begging the Dialect*, devoted only 49 of its 95 pages to short poems; the remainder of the book was occupies by a sequence of long ballads later given their own book, *Wordsong* (Sono Nis Press, 1983) with additional material. My next collection, *The Dark Window* (1962) devoted 35 pages to the title poem and 12 pages to translations of Tristan Corbiere, leaving only 49 pages for shorter poems. I came to Canada in 1963 and it was not until 1968 that I was able to find a Canadian publisher for my work. During those years I published two tiny collections of verse on Irish themes from the Dolmen Press, Dublin, and two even smaller chapbooks in Britain. Jack McLelland came to my rescue in 1968 and published *Selected Poems 1947-1967* containing only 23 previously uncollected poems. In 1969 my British collection, *Answers,* contained only 18 poems and when *The Hunting Dark* was published in both U.K. and Canada in 1971 it did not include many long completed poems because their style did not fit well with newer work. My next substantial collection of this period *Timelight* (1974) proved to be an unsuitable collection for many lyrics dealing with sex and love; a good many of these found a place in *Because of Love* (1977) but by no means all, my editor preferring less extreme attitudes than some into which my poems had led me. I have put the majority of these love poems into this book, as I have also included other poems whose harshness makes them appear the mavericks of my herd.

In the first version of this book I included 25 poems that had not previously appeared in books; in this edition I have added a further 39. In making my selection I have tried, nevertheless, to be rigorous as well as to be just to the man who wrote the poems, a man I sometimes have difficulty in recognizing. I have revised some poems very slightly but have not altered the tenor of any poem, and I have discarded none because I now disagree with or even dislike the attitudes it presents. One must be true to history, even one's own.

In conclusion I must express my debt of gratitude to Chris Petter of the McPherson Library of the University of Victoria and also and most especially to Ann MacLean. Had she not brought order to the confused mass of papers that I unloaded on the library I would never have discovered these poems and made this book.

Robin Skelton
Victoria,
British Columbia
1992

Overture

OVERTURE

Listen. This is
desperate. Listen.
I am the nervous
start in the dark
before sleeping,
the knee jerking,
the twitch of the lip
at a dreamed kiss,

and hide in your finger
as you touch
her breast or pick
the brush, the pen,
the razor turning
your wet cheek
and straining throat
to the lick of time.

I am confession,
the itch, the tic,
the morning erection,
the slow qualm
filling the belly,
the knees' tremble,
everything unintended,
known

only slowly
and known hidden,
the bones in the closet,
the lost names,
the dangerous memories,
the outrage
hidden and laughing
behind the house.

Shall I tell you
I am a liar?
You know that.

You know, too,
my lies are your lies,
your discoveries.
Have you remembered
that girl's name—

the one with the little
breasts that sat
across you, giggling?
Do you recall
the smell of her armpit,
her bad tooth?
Listen to this disc—
they were 'records'

then when you heard it
first. Do you
remember the sea-sick
lurch of the gut
at such beauty,
the sweet sadness,
calling that vomit
'our tune'?

Do you? Do you?
I remember
everything now.
The bones upstand.
Does it matter
if mine or yours?
Names are the first
things we pretend,

but not the most
important. Listen.
This is desperate.
I am trapped
in memory's riot,
carried through
everything that
bones lay claim to.

When I Began

THE MARK
(Rhupunt)

When I began
I was a man
released by dark,

then, given sight,
worked in the light
to make my mark,

which fades away
day by worn day
for all my sweat

that I may learn
I must return
and will forget.

RESPONSIBILITY

Year by slow year I
am causing my childhood;
when it is all constructed
I will die.

Understanding this,
I wish to pierce
my hand with nails
in anguish for that prisoner

running through the grass
tall as his head and sobbing
at the baying
of the loping dogs,

climbing the thorn tree,
shouting to his heart
Be Still! Be Still!
until I bring him stillness.

THE RED HOUSE

Sudden as a mirror, the red house
jumped from behind fluffed trees;
windowed four-square and flat-slated,
violet as final clouds, it seemed,
(or was, so solid its broad gesture),
a brick god chapped with litanies.

And there I was born, not I, but rather
the name of my face, the learned, caught
habits of sufferance: below
the slope of the narrow roof were formed
the tribal totems that hard words
have since tabooed, evaded, sought.

Come on it suddenly as a mirror
there at the road's turn, it was so
locked and fenced that, a blank neighbour
caught in an intimacy he knows
outside his role, I watched a boy
at last turn on his heel and go.

ANCESTORS

Tame jackdaw on his head, my father
lived boyhoods of stolen apples,
pawky curates, and drunk farmers;
slingshot in stackyards fed his owls
caged in the loft. Jack, black
as the ace of spades, mocked all comers,

made away once with a man's watch,
(none of your trinkets, a gold hunter
well cased and fobbed), was at last lost
and no heart to catch another.
Tales of the Wolds. My father's tales,
his father being the schoolmaster.

Those were titanic years still

in the Nineties. My Grandad's first bike
was the first for the Wolds. Some bad spills.
At an advanced age he learned Greek
to tease the parson, at service time
followed the lesson by the Book.

It was he, too, sending the boys off
to gather strawberries, said 'Whistle!
If you stop once, I'll be along!'
No aphorism of an apostle
or phrase of a great man ever struck
so firm as that legendary tattle.

And his father? The tale stops.
I only know he had many sons
and some daughters that took his wealth,
and there are some shaky tales that run
on how he brought rail to the east coast,
but, I think, garbled. Of details none.

So the story ends in a figure big
with the upland mist, who could trace back
himself, no doubt, to a great house.
There was money once, it is said. But Jack
is the clearest image. He thieved time
as my father apples, way back

there in the place where whistling proved
a trick of the innocence they loved.

RICHES

The ditch in Humber Lane
was black with tadpoles, round
black beads and whippy tails;
I knelt down at the side
and filled my jar as black
as now I fill this page,
glad of the gathered life,
however many died.

THE CIRCUMCISION

Smell the nice scent, she said. The table slithered
under my back on the blanket. I was ashamed
as I had been taught to be ashamed. The Doctor
held sweetness to my nose until the ceiling
swam and buckled, became a mist, sea-mist
shifting over the details of the mind,
and voices gathered distance. From far off
a small sharp pain pierced what I must not touch,
and my gut contracted. Half awake,
I shivered to the brutal, soothing words.

Cracks on the ceiling mapping a country of mist,
a snowscape stained by yellowing smears of time,
what should hurt, hurt.
      The tangible shame came home
suddenly, bandaged, ludicrous, alarming.
It was a 'thing'. (There were no words to use
except the disallowed.) A 'thing' I mustn't
see in a mirror, show to anyone, mention,
but only use, of necessity, on my knees
above the equally nameless shining porcelain
vivid with bluebirds on the rim, pink-breasted,
wide-winged, wide-beaked, flying . . .
      Wide-beaked, flying,
I lay in the mists of my bed to the sound of the sea
and the distant spectral voices. I flew. I faltered.
Gradually round my bed the shapes of air
solidified: my mother, her nurse-faced sister,
pulling the bedclothes back.

                                He isn't crying
but singing! (my mother's voice) *He's only singing.*
You're only singing, aren't you? I sang my crying,
hearing the tension twang in her throat, the laughter
of something frightened nearing, the eyes like
          gimlets,
and stitch by stitch by stitch and shame by shame,
the ceiling a sheeted mirror, the door concealment,
the curtains clogging the sky, the song explained

my loyalty to her terror, and cried my own.
I wept my terror. Then everything slowly, slowly
altered its dark perspectives. Upon my knees
I saw shame hurt for being shameful, pitied
what I could not love, nor yet protect,
and, mirrored back in urine, watched my features
shift and shiver, cramped upon my knees
praying to something other than the God
I knew from bedtime and the blur of sleep,
something nameless, vivid, mortal—someone
accepting the strange sweet smell, the ceiling
       buckling
the twisting shapes in the air, not Mother or Father,
but what has been always nameless, private, holy,
the shaming of shame by the human, the peace of
       the wound
discovered, the mirror transforming,
       but singing not crying.

THE LADDER

A long white room as cobwebbed as the sea;
I climbed there one morning, spell on spell,
for doves and apples, from the strawcrossed yard
rose on my muscles, head strained back to tell
how farther, nearer, all grew, near and far
holding the roar of wakening like a shell.

A gaunt door ribbed and knotted as a moor;
my hands rose up towards it, spell by spell,
in greed and wonder, heard the hinges groan
idly at nothing, as if they could tell
me all one day, but now were old; far down
a fallen feather, a black pool on the stone.

A long white room, a black pool on the stone;
I climbed up one morning, spell on spell,
in fear and courage, from the bruising yard
rose on my terrors, head strained back to tell
how room and fallen feather, near and far,
swung me between their twin reefs like a bell.

THE TOP
for Barbara Jump

Strain the cord round, tight as breeches
under the wall's lee, pull and curl
its staggering arc still, spun asleep
this city morning bright with rain;
so earth revolves; the leaf, now born,
now fallen, spins and is the same.

Fling wide arms out; sky-eyed as summer
in the hopscotch street, spin round until,
blurred as a top, the street is locked
in otherwhere, until the walls
slow into sickness; on their sides
the dead leaf and the top lie still,

And then again, the leaf, the top,
the body, spinning till their sleep
blurs time to that eternal poise
each prayer demands but cannot keep
one mortal morning. Wet with sun,
life, death, revolve and are the same

only at that point of rest.
We strain our cords, and pull, and lift
each staggering arc towards its sleep,
but cannot stay. Dream, deed, belief
slow into sickness, into time;
the world returns and is the same.

GREEN APPLES

In the rank orchard of a house
half-ruined, battered as a shoe's
gape from the dry ditch, but in use,
an old man's raging violent voice
hits at our heart-thuds, his abuse
sharper than sour of the green apples.

Hate, like a snake in the dusk's warm
gather of leaves gave a sin's name
to the jump of the breath in the breast bone
and the falter at sudden branches grown
crooked to nudge. It was not shame
or terror that set us on the run,

rather surprise that the old dark,
grumbling and warm, could flash light, break
stillness to spit such venom, took
hold of our minds. It was awake,
raucous; our robbery, mistook,
twisted into a different task.

In a far dry ditch: *He was proper mad;*
Do you think he saw us? We had not made
words for such falls, could not have said
how a hidden fable in all we did
was comfort, kindred, and one lad
dropped them for setting his teeth on edge.

ANGEL

They called her 'Angel', sardonic
at bitter scrubbing arm
sharp as a scraped white shinbone
there in the chicken run
for hens to clack at, mottled
brown by the rain and sun.

She was the sour-faced snatcher
at every gossip's tale,
bent graceless, thankless, angular,
over the clanging pail,
the wet wood rough with scrubbing,
the hot carbolic smell.

Yes, she was bitter, God knows—
bitter and sour and quick
to vex as a thistle blurting
its milk at a swung stick;
her head was a mortification
of curlers and twisted grips.

So 'Angel' they called her, laughing.
Her son was a big lad,
simple and shy and clumsy.
If ever she had a glad
softness for him she kept it dark,
abused all the luck she had.

And died. But before that last
vengeful retort to breath
she saw him wed and settled.
'Poor Angel' they said at his wreath.
And the women removed the tight curlers
once she lay small in death.

LONG-DISTANCE RUNNER

After the first two miles there is only a body
running upon hard earth past irrelevant tress,
watchful of nothing, attending to its own breathing,
eyes empty and chill as metal, thought released.

Nothing persists but persistence. Though there may be
a curlew whistling, a dog in a frost-grey yard,
a ploughman giddy with gulls, cries from the distance,
vermilion blurs of roofs by the far faint road

over against the canal or sidling the airfield's
windy desolation, and, elsewhere, friends
lovers, children, none of these things can matter;
only the body matters, the mindless blind

insistent throat of air, the compulsive lungbeat,
habitual muscles travelling the steady jolt
and pound of hard-packed byways; time only matters
for its obstinate pace by pace retreat,

its grudging admiration of an endurance
pure enough to depend on no profound
intent or oracle, thinking it sufficient
to concentrate on covering the ground.

WESTFIELD LANE

Westfield Lane, a green switchback
humping and scooping towards the wild
flat of the land north of the dyke
by Marsh Cottage; remembering that,
and, clearly, the saddle's jolt, the spin
of the blurred spokes, and the meshed ruts
tangled at gateways, remembering too
blue sky and boyhood, I begin
counting days back; an abacus
of worlds clicks on my natal string

five, ten, fifteen years back
till Westfield Lane, a scoop and climb
of green between the swaying fields
propels me down into the slack
lands round the deserted house;
dark in this brightest day, it looms
cold and decrepit. The door yawns
at a garden scrawled with a few trees
flayed by salt winds. Just beyond,
the rank dyke threatens the last field,

and beyond that an eight-mile waste
of grey water stirs and waits.
Looking back at Westfield Lane

the eye has altered, the light passed.
The house echoes. I mount and ride
the other road, by graveyard and stack,
home through the silent village square,
chilled and listening. That track
led me too far into my need,
and yet a new need drags me back.

LONG MAN'S QUARRY

The sliding planes of stone, the stacked
stone whiteness cliffed about a space
whose flat arena is cross-tracked
by scars of dead machines is mapped
as Long Man's Quarry. Some Long Man,
(no doubt) first found or made the place.

He came up from the matchboxed black
and higgledy-piggledy-alleyed town
down there, and struck out a new track
through time and tangle, and his luck
happened upon a place where white
gleamed through the thin turf of the down.

Six foot and more, his brown face dry
with the white smokes of dust his heart
disturbed in every thought, his eye
blinded and blue, he saw the way
to carve pure desolation, shape
the abstract nothingness of art.

Today the last machine has hauled
its last long parallel and gone,
leaving the scoured white stacks of walls
without a meaning save the tall
surrounded emptiness, the death
remote and blazing in the sun.

ADMISSION ONE SHILLING

At the end of the avenue, the house,
remote, affected by a disused grace,
accepts each tourist as half-recollected,
yet leaves a mild surprise upon the air
as if a menial coughed, or a guest's stare
at Vandyk or at Lely were intercepted.

This is disaster few can recognise,
undramatic, shaped by its own poise:
the terrace, carved as music, has no words.
Unstirring draperies of each stone Apollo
fold their time who made no sign of horror:
the sentinel elm is loud with omening birds

and ivy crawls at the pane; through pewter air
soot falls in benediction, each smudged star
etching the walls, whose hours accept endurance,
lost in the unalterable poise
of an illusion: how should we expose
their histories, who have not their assurance?

AS I REMEMBER IT

As I remember it, the place was old;
a fingernail pressed home into the wood
black-wet with autumn could scoop yellow cheese
that squashed like pith of elder in the hand;
wood-shavings, pitch-pine mostly, lay around,
the top layer fresh and crispy, faintly rose,
the ones below brown, sodden. Saw and axe
lay on a fruit box with a sharpening stone,
and everything was still. As I remember,
trees drooped stiff outside, and there was rain.

The Shed, they called it. 'Gone down to The Shed'
answered most callers of an afternoon.
Beyond the kitchen garden where the mud
from heavy boots had tramped the grasses down
to make a track, it sagged beneath the wind,
lopsided, flapping felt along one edge
of the half-hearted roof. The window—square
as nothing else was square—had on its ledge
a jam jar and five rusty nails a nudge
would always loose upon the stamped clay floor
among the shavings. On a hook a sickle,
rusted beyond belief, rocked at the door's
imperfect closing. Now I think of it,
there was a postcard pinned upon the door.

As I recall, it was from foreign parts—
I think a square with pigeons and a sky
more blue than possible, all shine and gloss,
and ill-shaped people promenading by;
the front was scratched, one corner tattered; why
the thing was pinned there heaven only knows.
As I remember it, I pulled it down.
It's odd how a chance memory grows and grows.

The card was at the back of it. The card
it was that set me thinking of The Shed,
and yet I almost missed it—small and bright,
its drawing pins rusted home into the wood.
The other side told nothing. All it said
was 'With Best Wishes' and the name was blurred
beyond all understanding, while the stamp
had gone long since. The whole thing was absurd.
And yet, as I picked up the nails again,
I felt a private glory had occurred.

THE FISHERS
for my Father

We melted down remnants of armies in the tin cup
shoved in the red of the fire, and chalked a spoon,
and poured the thin grey spelter in the spoon;
new, it shone like silver pocked by rain:
we carried it to the clays at the edge of the sea.

The fish were still that day. The brown line stung
our hands with the salt of its speed, and the grease of clays
shifted under our feet. The breakers came
and went and came; we swung, reeled in, and swung,
the silver flashing out into the brown
and salt-flecked lurk of waiting till our eyes
were harsh with salt and sun, our fingers cold.
There was no virtue in us day-long, none.

It might have been the image of the thing
caught us and fastened us down in places where
the big fish bite, the worn paint of the soldiers
marring the spelter with a touch of blood,
or maybe it was just not weight enough.

We had no good as fishers of those men.

LAND WITHOUT CUSTOMS
for John Montague

My land had no customs. Habits, tricks
of the slow tongue, leading beasts to grass,
roads slape with rain, or answering
weddings and deaths in a dry voice
scurfy as dust in the village square,
boys' names carved into the old stocks,

these—but no customs. Unless you count
the old men making one stretch of wall
the place for their backs, spring sun
blinking their eyes; or the way all
was marbles one day, the next tops
in the road alongside the brick school.

Certain inevitables there were: the rub
of hands on apron at house door
to speak to strangers, the mild horse
surging the plough at a harsh roar
of ritual violence, the long silence
before speech. And these were
known and unknown. The land stood
somewhere inside them. A phrase missed,
a nod too easy, and boots dragged
at embarrassed cobbles. Two miles west
it was shallower, lighter. I once saw
a man there run for the town bus.

But no customs. In a way stronger
for that, I think. There was no need
to assert the place. It grew, changed;
the electric came and a new road
out to the south, and the telephone.
The pump was condemned. But the past stood.

And I daresay still, in its own way,
stands. Though a plaque by the old stocks
set in the wall is a thought strange,
there in the square are the old looks,
the pause before speech, the drab men
spitting in dust. Should I go back

these will have made me. The small fields
are as small elsewhere, the sky as blue
or just as grey with a thread of rain,
the stacks as lumpish, but here grew
something inalienable, a way
of giving each least thing its due,

a rock to living. A land without
customs, yes, but a land held
hard on its course, unsparing, firm
in its own ways. As I grow old
time hardens into that sure face
watching the foreign, shiftless world.

JOHN ARTHUR

John Arthur walks the tideline-scribbled sand,
having nothing else to do but let things slide,
driftwood, wreckage, weed kicked into mounds,
poked and prodded, taffled and let bide.

You'd think, his tar-smeared rain-stained mac
flapping at every slouched lunge of the knee,
he had a wisdom that we strangers lack,
some slow-tongued gnomon of sand, wind, and sea,

and was content. You'd think that if you could,
unwilling to believe him derelict,
walking beside great waters whose brown flood
roars down a wreckers' harvest to be picked—

kindling (of course) its staple, but much more
washed from the fat black coasters as they roll—
you'd figure him an uncrowned ignorant Lear
trapped on the blustered edges of the world,

and you'd be wrong all through, because John Arthur
has nothing else to do but let things slide;
driftwood and sunlight, weed and wanting, slither
endlessly through him like the sour brown tide,

and days are just for filling in with time.
Get closer and you'll see his sandblind stare.
One foot drags, one hand twitches, waves crash down
and mile and mile on mile destroy the shore.

LETTER TO AN IRISH POET

to John Montague

Our trades being one, across the sea
I'd send a ring of stones
to share your field; their history,
weathered and worn, each turning day
stands round my name, their great jawbones
clamped, imprisoning me.

John was the slacklipped village one
that showed unbuttoned flies;
harshly warned by the dark woman
never to meet with him alone,
I had terror of his huge cow eyes,
fear of his wrist bone.

George, wordless, knew the weather's way,
taking his beasts to grass
shirt-sleeved or coated before the day
knew its own mind, sun, wind, or rain
assured by how his body was,
slow in the deep lane.

Jack, in his tarred warped boards of shed
more tender than any girl,
eyes blue lights in his bear's head,
bent sweat and bristle to my boyhood,
nodded and growled—nets, ropes, furled
salt on his walls. And he, too, dead.

Three men of all. Across the sea
I'd send three towering stones
of the huge ring their history
makes part and, fastened on to me,
holds me to earth where, breath and bone,
my first words learned to be.

But how leave such land anchorage?
Held fast in the jaws
of a mantrap forged in our first age

when faith began, can grief or rage
unloose the clamp? And is there cause
to harrow up our lineage?

THE BRIGG

It was six foot four of my father
balanced upon the jag
of the green-brown rock with his bright rod
after the long drag
round from the bay over weed-raked pools
that made me see the Brigg.

His hair was white as the flying spume,
his hand as hard as wood,
his eyes blue as the blue pool
that mirrored how he stood,
holding within its depthless rock
sky-space, man, and flood.

Inverted there like a totem hung
down into the sky
where spectral gulls involved the weed
with gaping soundless cry,
he fished a far unbeing sea
no man might profit by.

I watched him, back towards the pool,
cast out into the foam
beyond the ledge of rock on rock;
I watched him stand alone,
one man as tall as any tower,
and one deep as stone.

THE WALLS

Straddled the walls, then ran like lemurs
along the curved copestones, weather-flaked,
cement like breadcrumbs, height of a man
above the playground; sometimes stuck
there on the high bit, but scrambled down,
reddening the good clothes, grazing skin.

That equilibrium was our track,
our livelihood's leap, and our way round
playground and school. We could turn back
only to hide or ambush. Walls
were the only roadways, to walk flat
on grass or asphalt no walk at all.

Places to miss: the girls' playground lav
with its climbable walls taboo, the boys'
bogs that stank and were scrawled with love
a different omission; we climbed round
or sidled through nettles, breath sharp,
rather than tackle the bad ground.

Cheating you might say. But then each
scurry along the six-foot edge
of the highest wall was a kind of cheat;
or the clutch and balance on one brick ledge
in the school wall itself; or the leaping down
by the sycamore branch to the hay field;

everything cheating death, deceiving
everything else. Where They looked, there
we were almost never; Their voices came
crazily over the blue air;
we straddled a barrier somewhere else
beyond them, freed of love or blame.

And thus all summer, all one summer long,
three of us running. A new game
that taught us (we knew, but we did not know
just how we knew) something that shamed
and frightened, a thing that was seek and hunt,
risk and deceive. In the pit below

one corner where boughs drooped (deeper there
the fall from the wall) I crouched once,
hearing the call. It repeated, stopped.
I had run two walls from its first blast
and was in my hide-out. No-one came.
Doors slammed. The universe was vast.

PLUMS

An old man picking plums—
well, not so old,
say seventy-three or so—
leans, stilted tall,
upon his long green ladder,
pulls through leaves
and gaps of sky and
knuckled twigs and pulls
all afternoon. You just
can't call him down
whatever call you try.
Try fear. Try prayer.
Try rattling ice in glasses.
One branch more
is just beyond him still,
lumped huge with plums
he nods with, sways with,
tugging ripeness free
for all our hesitations
and our love,
still learning how it feels,
how plum trees feel
and fingers on the plums
to cries of *Please,*
no higher! Careful there!
Don't fall! He's got
his eye in now;
he'll pick till it is bare.
Which isn't what we'd planned
for him, and isn't

what he thought himself
when he got up
among the lower branches,
but it makes
the world redeemable;
he just can't stop.
When you grow plums
you have to get them down.

APPLE LOFT

Whether the quiet breaks us, or we the quiet,
there is a listening in the apple loft,
spread webs powdered from the whitewash-slap
dead in corners, beams with rivulets
and seams of grey, and finger-holes and cracks,
and apples, apples, apples, making smell
something as definite as the way the wood
knocks on the elbow when you start to crawl
where the eaves let daylight in, and should
you touch one it is certain to touch back,
not like a proper apple that you pick
and bounce between your hands and catch and bite,
but like a cheek that won't twitch when you touch
but still reminds you, *This belongs to me,
so watch your fingers now.*You move away,
not only as you've been told not to bruise
or even climb there, but as there's no use
to pretend this quiet has no say—
it's all so full of saying. Dust is loud
always, of course, when it lies thick on wood
over the bending head, and cracks of light
are always talking inwards to the pit
of shadow under them, and white webs swing
a leaning rocking drymouthed sort of song
and the beams croak. But the apples here
are quieter and sharper on the ear;
waiting explosions tensed upon a hush
of triggered whispering, they will surely breed
in blazing stillness their own way of speech
to the last letter; as the loft turns round

its store of muttering, they touch each hand
that touches with a warning that to reach
too soon is to find everything turned sour,
and silence useless. Let them lie and wait,
assured with ripening. Why should we destroy it?
Sooner or later life speaks out—too late
for quiet keeping or for keeping quiet.

CART FRANK

Rattle and jolt of the cart
was all his day; he went
village by village through
the flat and green land, bent
over a slack rein, nodding
at ways the hedges leant.

Children, women, chickens,
drunkards, boxes, sacks,
under the hooped green canvas
flapping at his back,
travelled ten miles of gossip
to his whip's crack.

And yet no haste was made,
the whip and the hoarse shout
simply props of the play
their journey acted out
to the last cramped stretch
of leg, the stamping foot

upon the platform edge
where, massive, hustling, black,
the brute of revolutions
rimmed on its iron track
snarled steam like a house-dog,
and the cart turned back.

Rattle and squeal of axle
then at the day's end meant
prayers for the heart's acceptance,
old bones dry and bent
over a slack rein watching
ways their memories went.

JOE SAMPSON

Waistcoat wrinkled brown as puddles,
chin scattered with bristling white,
cheeks red as good meat,
long gun under arm, he'd shot
the fox, caught it along the hedge
of North Field End, and watched it drop.

In another country no reason
could have protected him—a bitch
heavy with young at that time of the year!
But Joe Sampson cleared thistle, vetch,
and fox with the same plough-logic; here
land must be conquered at all's cost.

Something there was in him honest, crude
as the turned clay's shined swerve
back of the plough, and something mocking
the cluttered sentiments round the grave
of any vermin, or used thing;
guns are beliefs a man must have,

each death a clearance of good land
and the land's decision. None were
boxed but rightly; none lived
except by land-rule. He closed the door
of the Bull, and leaned his shotgun up,
slapped the brush down on the bar.

MESSAGE FOR MY FATHER

I'm never certain what the message is
except that it is quiet and in words.
I watch you bending by the apple tree,
the white cloud massive as a watching head,
the dark earth gentle. Maybe time compels.
Or maybe time is all we have to spare.

I used to climb, once, a particular tree
under a stack side, and its upper twigs
wore crazy straws clawed from that stack I'd slide
and slither down most days, adept at falls
on to the gold ground, breathless, jumping up
to climb again and slide down from the sky.
But the tree. I think that it was bare,
or nearly bare, the mossed bark knuckled through,
the twigs dry. Certainly there were no apples.
Yet it lived. Transfigurations talked
crowded as sparrows in its bitten leaves.
If it had leaves. I can't remember quite.
Yes, leaves there must have been, for there was shade
poppling my face in sunlight. I would pick
one leaf and keep it like a word from home.

And so it comes round to it, slowly round,
nearing the message—if the leaf will speak,
if words and memories can be retrieved.
You're standing now, and easing your stiff back,
watching the Worcester Pearmains change the sky.
Yet how am I to say...what can't be said
except by silence? I talk silence out
until it comes back filled with every phrase
of hesitation, every false start,
the passion, the inquiry, and the love.

In Times of War

SONG OF HONOUR

for Herbert Read

I

The inventor of
barbed wire was
thinking of cattle.

My brother lay there
tripes skeined out
like silk.

II

A question of
weight of
manpower,
         cannon-fodder:
Falstaff and
Talleyrand
watch us
    filling the pit.

III

Passionate fear of
pity is also
pity

eating away the
vitals like a
fox.

IV

We do not live,
We die aloud

to flags and oaths.
The centuries

steal our graves.

BIG FIELD

Who will read this? Many of them are dead.
The white Pavilion on Big Field is gone,
and everything is altered but the heart
I hurt myself with; even the Drome is done,
ploughed-up, forgotten. *You've come back to look
the Old School over, then? They all come back.*

Even the tireless dead. A smell of sweat
lives in the changing rooms I crouched in, crying,
with a twisted arm; a smell of piss
drifts through the shrill-voiced bogs; my fingers smearing
dubbin are clagged yellow, gritted, sore;
I take the ball and fall; mud claws my nails,

and masks my jersey. *Stand up! Prove yourself!*
Prove that you're not a girl! He grabbed my towel.
That was during the Spanish Civil War
when everyone backed Franco. Thin and pale,
I was martyred small in a narrow bath
at ten years old. Shame is a kind of death.

He is a Doctor now, firm-voiced, assured
with sicknesses, and not among the dead
who came back huge with uniforms, and told
new dirty stories, and smoked cigarettes
openly in the corridors. On one wall
we kept a map of the fighting. When France fell

that summer I cried, walking to Big Field
to play twelfth man in a match that never ended.
It was a hot drugged day. Europe had stopped.
The Gods had lied, and Glory now pretended
that it hadn't meant it. Dreams went sick.
Nobody ever let me get to the wicket;

I stayed in the outfield always. There two boys
taught me the lesser death. The wind is cold
across Big Field, and in the spinney dark
trees gather round dark waters. Long ago
I stood here in my world and felt it crack.
You've come back, then, he said. *They all come back.*

CHAPEL HILL

Everything happens again.
    Behind the door
of an empty, broken house
    in a crumbling row
you pressed your body to mine.
    Is it true you are dead?
Your chestnut-red hair flares
    past this open window

of *The Feathers*. You're
    almost in the Square,
almost waiting.
    At the Seven-a-side
your brown eyes levelled at me
    and my heart thumped
up in the tightened throat.
    Girls weren't allowed.

My school cap burned my head.
    We walked together
carefully, without touching.
    The pavement was narrow.
Your breath had an
    impediment. I blushed,
stumbling, absurd, huge-limbed,
    one foot in the gutter,

astonished, terrified.
    I am still frightened
today in the echoing narrows
    between the tall
wall and the high tarred plank
    fence, where you stopped.
The kiss was a sudden furnace.
    My bones failed.

Your death won't remember my name,
    but I remember
saying your name, hot cotton
    upon small breasts,

lying on Chapel Hill,
        sun-drugged, my hand
moving slowly onto your
        pad of hairs;

and then awake in the
        dormitory, sighs
from rows of small beds, faint
        as ghosts. That summer
astonishment began
        in a ruined house,
your belly pressed hot on mine.
        Outside, grey rain

was the dangerous commonplace
        dream, where bombs had fallen
to give the house to us.
        One place we met
a Halifax crashed in the stream.
        They heard the gunner
screaming. The scar on the bank is
        brown there yet,

and, still, your back against the
        wall, I feel
you holding me more close
        than any mother
in the echoing narrows.
        On Chapel Hill
again I feel the chill in the
        hot summer

we never completed.
        I lie back on long grass
between the bushes and try to
        think your hand
and boldening hesitance.
        Bells called us home,
but left our imprint on
        the common ground.

THE MADRAS INCIDENT

In the station at Madras, he said *I am a Christian*.
His face was a yellow leaf and thin as a leaf.
His suit was white. Embarrassed, I brushed him off.

The beggar woman had no feet at all,
but a tumour big as a foot upon her stomach
shone like cattle hide. I stank with sweat.
The leg of the man by the gate was an elephant's leg.

Jao! Jao! Jao! I said, being very young,
and frightened most of the time, unable to give
without distaste because of the smell of fear.
The black Madrassi led the way with smiles.

And nothing outrageous happened. Nothing split
the tumour, burst the leg. No scalpel voice
came holy from the wolfish yellow face

that only tried to weep, and turned away.

REMEMBERING ESQUIMALT

*for Frank Fryett, who, after several years in
a Japanese Prisoner of War Camp near
Nagasaki, was repatriated to a Rehabilitation
Centre at Esquimalt on Vancouver Island.*

For rehabilitation
his camp was Esquimalt.
I remembered the kelp
in the tangling sea,
and the English gardens;
he remembered snow,
and eating meat, and
walking alone at night,

those years ago. V.J. Day
he'd seen a mirror.
"Christ," he said, "I'm
bent as a bloody crone!"

"You've had that crook back
all the bloody time
we've been in the mine!" they said;
he hadn't known.

And marching through Nagasaki,
"It looked like a flower
among the stones," he said,
"a cup and saucer
melted and hardened back
into folds of petals.
Lovely it was," he said,
"but I felt sick

thinking about it after."
We drank to Esquimalt,
all that clean blue air.
"One day," he said,
"on the ship from Java
we saw a tanker struck,
and the bastards burning and
running about like mad

ants, all burning whether
they jumped or not.
The sea was on fire," he said.
"We laughed and clapped
and cheered and stamped
to see the buggers trapped.
It isn't nice to think of
the way you get,

or even some things you've seen.
I liked Esquimalt.
They asked us to dances."
He picked up his stick.
"A bit like a rose," he said,
"I should have kept it.
That was one of the things
I should have kept."

BREAD

Off Massawa
the ship's ventilation failed.
It was hot as hell.
The assistant baker
pummelled dough till swagging dropsical bellies
flopped and slapped like seals.
He wasn't well,
had prickly heat like red ants crawling up
his hide from heel to neck.
Red-eyed, he swore,
This fucking war!
His girl was a five pound trick
on Lime Street, Liverpool, and all night shift
he bragged about the good times that he'd left.

Bread maddened us.
Unloading the deep oven
scorched skin to a desert.
Wrapped in sacks,
our hands played chuck and grab with loaves whose crusts
could cut us open.
Sweating cobs, we rapped
the black tins empty, clattered them in stacks,
and juggled, cursing, with the hissing loaves.
Five hundred bloody mouths!
the chief spat, hitching
up his gross white belly, fold on fold,
above another mix.
He weighed four hundred
pounds or more, and had a piglike eye.
His number three kept cheerful,
listed brothels
he could vouch for.
None of us could breathe

that hot night off Massawa.
Bread smells good
by loaves, but not by hundredweights.
We raved
by morning, kept

our eyes away from knives
that told how cleanly the soft firmness sliced
and tore when we tugged free damp parcels that
rose into plumpness sensual as the girls
we fingered every night,
rehearsing vice
on verbal rosaries, all words the same,
till dawn broke more heat out
and we lay slack
and flaccid as the bread
we'd never bake.

VIET NAM

I

We huddled under the stairs among wet raincoats
smelling of rubber. Fear had a rubber smell.
Rustle, crackle and slither quickened pulses
for an approaching climax that never came
except to others. Searchlights stroked the sky.
The dog lay trembling on my mother's lap.

Explosions all were distant. We learned the distance.
Wearily we dragged ourselves to bed
in the grey dawn light. Another warning
heard and useless. Almost we longed to fall
beneath the falling house, to climb out broken
into a world of drifting rags and dust.
Almost we longed to welcome what was nearing,
crump by crump, across the muddled fields,
haphazard giant steps; the windows rattled
kettledrums: he comes. . . . he Comes. . . . He Comes. . . .

Next morning we picked twisted iron fragments,
emblems, relics, kept them. They were nails,
the shards of martyrdom from which we'd hid
beneath the endless climbing of the stairs.

II

Twenty years ago. Old photographs.
Letters from the attic. Singapore
had fallen and altered every stamp collection;
I collected aircraft instead of moths.

The poetry does not matter. Ignore the poetry.
Europe, a rorshach test for the sick and mad,
slowly altered its meanings. . . . an iron bird. . . .
an inconceivable death. . . . a loaf of bread. . . .

It is not enough to be wise; one must be lucky.
Aesop was wrong as the card in the weight machine
in the summer of Munich. . . . Have you noticed
how the simple smell when they're burned alive?

III

Now there is war again. Protruding eyes
gaze into my face, find what's not there.
Hate! roared the Sergeant, beetroot-necked, *Put All
Your Weight Behind It—NOW—Lunge—In—Twist—Out!*
Horrible, O most horrible! We clung,
but desperation made us impotent,
huddling under the stairs. I pick my way
awkwardly through tributes to the dead,
recalling oil upon my fingers, hands
that slapped the bolt back, CRASH, then bruised the shoulder
stiff with webbing. *Hate!* the Sergeant yelled.
I was not fit. My fingers blurred with cold.
It is not enough to survive; one must have suffered,
thrust with all one's weight, and known the blind
reduction of the earth—Lidice, Dresden,
Ilium, Seoul converted into braille.

IV

Victory is my private nausea. Huddled
in an Indian Cinema, I was sick
all over the next seat. I celebrated
peace with vomit. Later, in the hills,
another victory and another drink.

All the years of eating hate and fear
ended in disgust. A cloud of locusts
settled on the hill below the camp,
each bigger than a soldier's severed thumb,
each louder than a bullet's whine. We played
tennis at the Governor's and I lost
again, again.
                    My father's old tin helmet
hangs upon the wall; my paybook lies
somewhere among the rubble in my drawer.
This time we're out of it. Another Leader
and another rabble beat the drum
and burn the villages whose children huddle
under palm thatch and the dripping leaves,
adepts of terror and the will to die,
as kettledrums of guns announce He Comes,
the Prince of Peace, the God, the Cloak of Fire,
the Great Society of all we are
who, blind and witless, huddle under stairs.

THE QUAKE

A mountain wrinkled
way up north.
        The heavy
night throbbed like a dynamo whose loose
bolts well might fly
high as the climbing stars
that swung and rocked upon their ladders.
                                    Dogs
cried out in human voices.
                        I held hard
to both sides of my slithering bed,
then kicked
the damp sheet off to stagger at a wall
that had moved closer, thinking me a dream
it could identify and share.

                        A voice
cried "Jesus Christ !"
                        A woman
wailed, as wind
threw solid air between the barrack blocks
and pushed breath to the edge.
                        "Outside," he cried,
but everyone held on,
braced stiffly,
trapped
by fear of the familiar,
                        could not run,
though tables ran like dogs
in hugger-mugger
yelping rabblement.
                        It was a mountain
wrinkling did it,
way up north,
        a mountain
no-one lived on
moved by private need
to counter deepening cold.
                        The lights came back.
We set the room to rights, swept up the glass.

It was a minor tremor; Death survived.

CHAKRATA

I have been there:
the cold mountain
pines drippy with
black rain,
the hard-mouthed ponies,
the straw-faced
visitors with
their rag bundles. . . .

To have been there
is to have been
alive, and to be

alive still.
Memory proves us.
We perform
acts to remember,
thin as mist,

guessing at mountains
that are mountains
only because we have seen
or dreamed
their black pines,
their straw-faced
visitors with
sapphires, diamonds.

THE WINDOW

Girl at a bright-lit window;
dust and heat
heaved and scratched the lung;
she had slow arms
lifting to coil the hair:
another figure
moved behind her,
a privileged hungry ghost.

Voyeurs both, we stared.
The back of the brothel
abutted on our huts.
By night the blinds
were shut; by day the windows
were empty glass:
only at twilight could
they hint, we guess

at the accomplished world
of Civilians Only.
The face of the girl
was nothing but a girl's

round unexciting face;
the hair was merely
hair, the arms
unglamorous, ordinary.

Yet the ghost
moved softly as a butler,
richly, blandly,
and, two ghosts in deepening
twilight, we stared on,
our flat grey air
framing that bright
multi-coloured square

before the blind shut
and the music, faint
as Paradise, began.
We kept our place
disconsolately, our eyes
upon the blind:
a sword-edged gateway
burned us in the face.

THE RELIQUARY
to Herbert Siebner

Our fathers were both Artillerymen,
both at Ypres.
Defeated, you were a prisoner,
and I the same
in my victorious desert.
In the still of the evening
we drink beer together.
I show you the box from home.
These are mutual relics:
glass from a shattered
chapel your father's guns
and mine both scored;
even this shrapnel,
bronze rust of a twisted leaf

fallen in Mametz Wood,
could have been shared.

My father kept everything;
we too have kept
somewhere among our nightmares
a childhood bond:
your German voice is that of a
fear grown friendly;
you are astonished that I am,
you say, "kind";

but, living on this island,
we drink together
in the still of the evening,
the box at our feet.
This half-burned wood
was part of a riotous victory
conflagration:
my father plucked it out.

There are notes in the box.
In the saps at Ypres
the rats ran away with our candles. . . .
I picked a stone
from the rubble of San Pierre Church
as a memento . . .
pocketed a plug . . .
cut a chip from a beam . . .

Ruin is our familiar.
To him it was strange.
Suddenly darkened by memories,
our minds veer
back to cities of fire,
a house unfolding
outward, suddenly peeling
itself to the core.
Nothing is ever forgotten.
We haunt the ghosts
we pack in boxes.
Here's a chunk of iron

the shape and size of my thumb
and marked *A piece*
that very nearly got me.
I wasn't born

the day this burned and
whistled past his ear
to split a sandbag;
nor were you; we both
derive from luck,
victim or seed of iron,
tricks of trajectory,
random errors of death,

a fortunate generation. . . .
You fill your glass
to yarns of a nightmare journey
across a moor,
the thin-jawed captain
watchful for retreat,
the unseen English
creeping round like fire;

and then the hospital train
torn up like cardboard,
the Russian nurse assigning
death or death
with one glance at your motions:
you clown your terrors,
laughing; we laugh
till we are out of breath

at such absurdities.
And yet today
headlines recur:
a Senator has declared
himself against *"The Left,"*
and rapturous crowds
have roared at his talk of *"The Enemy."*
This we endured
before, and have not forgotten
the shapes of death,

the trumpet note cut off high,
the wreaths black-green
against the scrubbed white stone,
the acres of crosses
planted where mankind died
for a song, a name,

a folly, a habit, a God. . . .
Our fathers crawled
the mud we crawled, and heard,
like us, the claim
of Truth for slaughter:
in this cardboard shrine
cold iron, burned wood, dead names
all weigh the same.

PETER

*In memory of my Indian Bearer
at Samungli, near Quetta, 1945-6*

Peter was nearly a rock:
on the shale and granite flank
of the dry brown mountain, lumped
with baked-clay blocks, he limped
order to whitewashed rooms.
Night came suddenly down
in that border country,
and at night we drank.

Few of us really died;
the worst was a camel laid
swollen across the track,
her unseamed belly-flaps
shaking at the sand
storms and the lion-maned
yellow dogs: shite-hawks
waited without pride.

Those dogs were hard to get,
knowing what was what

ran at a sniff of a gun;
I remember heaving one
into the nullah, huge
as a pony, almost grudged
the smeared beaks what I gave:
some bones may be there yet.

And Peter also died,
or acted as if he did,
went and didn't come back.
Often his old hands shook
and his eyes were raw;
only ten years before
the buildings had slithered down
and buried all he had.

Nineteen thirty-five,
and everything he loved
crumpled in thunderous dust
and altered to his past.
He used to go on the drink.
Who wouldn't? We all drank
in that place: it helped
to make it sense to live,

as he helped, patient, old
in his Imperial world,
serving and teaching the young
Sahibs the good customs,
long trusted and long kind.
One man went out of his mind
that Christmas with the drink;
we had to knock him cold.

And the camel so hard to shift
that it could only be left
for dogs and kites and sand. . . .
Some things stick in the mind
like prayerflags; on the other
hand, some don't: I bother
my head for Peter's face,
but have not lived enough.

THE MEMORY

We call it Memory.
                    Her arms are hard.
Light shadows half her face to make a mask
and ape Persephone. The bedclothes itch.
My fingers are as idle as her mouth.

That year in India, the month of madness
before the summer broke beneath its weight
and let the deep rain fall, dust clogged the skin
and bit into the throat. Her hands were spare

and quick as lizards flickering on the wall
to strike and shiver at the sweets of death.
I put my hands behind my head and yawn

the satiate yawn of love.
                    Outside, offshore,
a seal swerves glistening light and noses down
through rippling dark. The dark side of her face

is gentle as a pool; the other, lined
about the mouth and eyes, is kind and hard
as ivory, and the ivory six-armed dancer
by my bedside on the black wood base
shakes as I shiver.
                    Living takes its time
from dusts of memory dancing in the heat.

SERGEANT CASEY

Sergeant Casey called them fucking niggers.
Faces along the track were bubbles of kelp
glistening with sweat in the swimming heat.
Divers, we watched from the windows as they begged
all the way through the Punjab.
                    Sergeant Casey,
face flushed, beat them off.
                    Jao! Jao!

                                                    Their rags
were shreds of canvas ripped from long-wrecked ships.
Their bandaged heads wore cerecloths of the drowned.

And Casey unimaginatively knew
just what they were—
a threatening alien people.
Fucking niggers. Wogs.
He could not listen,
fearing the siren music of the damned
as energetically as he feared the least
original proposition, or the swollen
gland, the bloodshot eye:
these could destroy
virility with pity;
he would not pity ;
every strength was vulnerable in his world
and asked devout protection.
He was certain
of his air and element, aware
of all he could not breathe.
Three days we shared
the travelling narrows of the train, and swum
through dense sargassoes, fighting off the shoals.

I think of Sergeant Casey now, religious
in his purities, a noble man
appalled by suffering, knowing it the evil
pitch he must not touch.
I hear him damn
those torturing fathoms in a sweat-blind rage
of raw humanity and watch him down
his seventh pint,
show snapshots of his children
dancing in thc waves on Ventry Strand.

WAR NEWS

Death is Webster's territory. It helps
to think it literary. *What's this flesh?*
A little crudded milk. . . Her skin is silk,

my daughter's, as she staggers, stumbles, walks
three-four-five-six-and seven tongue-clenched paces
into worlds where poetry keeps us safely
in disguise from others and ourselves.
I make her poems. I make her gentle poems
against the shivering fevers of unease
that pierce imagination with the facts
of skin in jellying flame, of children's games
that torture children. . . . "Bang you're dead! You're scalped.
And I've cut off your ear." Her leaking bear
bashed hard against the playpen doesn't squeak
as she squeaks when she falls. *Her fault and beautie*
blended together shew like leprosie,
this human thickening, this gradual change
of hands to stumps clamped upon gun or pen,
and I cry, "You've hurt Teddy! Love poor Teddy!"
Hypocritically, she mimes tears,
hugs like a strangling *member of that noble*
and free league of amitie and love
we offer those we help into the pit
and count among our playthings. It is fit
here, facing innocence, to see its game
of brutal happiness and grief as foreground
for the other imagery of the screen,
the blurting smoke-clouds, the distorted dead,
who lie like dolls within the playpen bars,
eyes clicked wide open, limbs tugged off, squeaks gone. . . .
Vertue, where art thou hid? What hideous thing
is it that doth eclipse thee? Merely human
kind, mere humankind. She cannot be
more than she's born. Here, baby-faced, these burn
dolls' houses, comforted that nothing's real
except the urge to stagger, stumble, walk
into applause and adulthood. I bless
her small head, marvelling, and hide my fear
of human fear, of human love, this race
that kills its kind like dolls, and soldiers on
to labour upright in a falling room.

CONSIDERING ULYSSES

Climbing up from the boat, he must have figured
a good part of his act, walked easy, slow,
wouldn't you say? He was no fool. He knew
the score all right, knew what the world had asked for.

Much of the myth remains, but hardly all.
Lying abed under piled skins after the day's
inconclusive skirmishing, did he smoothe
the bone of his brow, the white length of his muscle,
quieting them like hounds? Did his eye catch
reflection-patterns of water on the canvas
making his heaven swim, then part the flaps,
breast into night and stars from shaking waves?

Fires on the beach we know about. Charred wood
black on the scratched beach. Myriads of fires.
Dried weed mounded on forks humped over shoulders
oily with sweat. Blanched driftwoods of dead spars
making walls for their backs. And we can guess
the way they skipped stones idly across the waters,
waiting, as everyone waits, harsh sounds of honing
counterpointing hushes of the sea.

So much we can guess, and how he lay,
mind still, resting his sex, till under his fingers
a woman, and then a horse, were traced in sand
and it was figured out. I'd say he knew
then, as sure as God made little apples,
how to fix it: planks, clamps, gilt, paint, nails . . .
There upon the beach, hock-deep in foam,
it stood how many cubits high? We know
the rest, the burning, pillage, rape, but not
how then he lay back, slept, arranged his hands,
traced giants, wars, storms, girls, nor if he saw
behind his days the fraying tapestry.

EPILOGUE

After the struggle
it is not
the weariness
but the strength
appals,

the taut compulsion,
the contingent stance,
remembered weight upon
the idle arms

accusing nakedness,
the gesture stiff,
and jargon,
grown familiar on the tongue,

recalling Victory
or Defeat
as if
they were not finished
and they were not one.

The Undefeated Dead

VIRGINIA ROAD REVISITED
In memory of Wilfred Childe

Twelve years ago.
Nostalgia silts the mouth
with smoke and stale beer,
shutting down the eyes
under the black slate weight
of roofs in rain,
blunting the finger-ends
with brick in streets
that step through puddles.
Here's where I was young,
paused at the corner
for a last look up,
then left him along
cobbled laurelled roadways.

Virginia Road.
All much as I remember.
The hollow shabby rooms,
chairs grouped round smoke,
drab walls, and settling dust.
Right at the top
he had a room we'd meet in
once a week,
hunched by the stuttering
broken columned gas
that itched our ankles,
on the mantlepiece
Blake postcards, snaps,
a child's small Union Jack.

He's gone now. Memories
cover him like frost,
hardening the hard clay.
He, as much as youth,
slid past, and still
slides past, without allowing
love its liberties.
I scrub my breath
round on the window, and

glare out. The laurels
shake their mockery.
The gas fire's cough
and whisper has the roaring
lungs of death.

No portrait can account
for him, no verse
mumble him wise enough,
or muffle up
the bad teeth in the
secret impish mouth
he talked from once
a week there at the top
of dark uncertain stairs,
books lumped and piled
on chairs, shelves, tables
and the clumsy floor.
Men climbed to see him.
Pride lay small but sharp

among the books and
solitudes. Twelve years!
I stare, red-eyed, through
fog and bid him come,
my old companion,
thrusting back the rest.
The trench of shadow
lies across the gloom
of cobbles. Lamps gasp out.
Rain starts. I watch
him wind the long wool
from his waking throat
and settle, listening,
in this upper room

I struggle to up stairs
of years, and pause,
my mouth still thick with breath.
He smiles. The gas
roars infinites of rain
and grief, its heat
pressed home upon our

lungs. I stare across
black weights of roofs.
No oracles assert
our laurelled frenzy,
but his need is mine;
books tumble and flags wave
our mutual loss.

DIRTY SNOW

In memory of William Robins and Jacob Kramer

Dirty snow at the base
of the grey-black statue
of the Prince,
in Leeds that year he blew
whiskey through his hands,
(I talk of Jacob).
Now he is dead as his
father on his slab.

Of the wrong race
to mourn, I can't lift
hands high, cloth backsliding
from sharp wrists;
I drink beer slowly
in the Jubilee,
thinking about my Grandfather,
who was blind,

dirty snow in his eyes;
"On the way," he said,
"Stop the hearse at the Hildyard Arms;
have one on me."
None of them did, of course.
I drink to Jacob,
who took his brush to the dead
and trusted grief.

His father, humped and scooped
in limestone, lay
stiff on the slab,

(*A Painting of my Father*) ,
like huge-skulled Delius,
his angered cheekbones
taut with parchment,
(*Head of Delius*),dead.

Brown snow under my boots,
in Leeds that year
he bent his huge-nosed, flushed,
imperial head
in smoke-fogged, comfortable
bars. Old snow
slid underfoot. Beer glistened
pools of wood.

Great names, great myths
amused his heavy eyes
and twitched the mumbling
confidential mouth,
the scraped, white-speckled chin,
his big red hand
heavy upon my
uninstructed mind.

Snow on his eyes,
"Have one on me," he said.
"Stop at the Hildyard Arms."
I didn't know
him dead till he was buried.
Jacob also
slid into the rivering dark
without a word
and altered the tides of the sea.
The statue looms
black horse, black rider, to
grey sky, where snow
won't fall from now.
Uneasy Spring begins
its muddled sentiment.
No dead awake.

THE COME-BACK

I walk my reappearance
round these streets
with a familiar terror.
What remains
could be more than it was.
A greasy pavement
slithers my nervous feet
in expected rain.
Mount Preston. The
Particular Baptist Chapel.
The flat was, surely,
a little further on.

It smelt of cat and gas;
my unmade sheets
stayed on the bed for wceks;
I never made
real contact with the laundry;
my clothes were damp
and baths impossible:
you'd think that I'd
still recognize it, but
they look the same.
One of the three is
boarded up and dead.

That could be it. But
then, perhaps not. I can't
re-live what might be
somewhere else. I'm locked
out properly here;
impossible to claim
nostalgia for a house that
will not look
familiar, for all the
times it gripped
me in dark hallways.
Quickly, I turn my back,
uneasiness nearing dread.

"It isn't fair"
sounds like a child's whine
in my head. I trace
out doubt a route towards
the echoing rock-
encrusted house at the corner
of Cromer Terrace;
my basement room's still there;
I stoop and peer.
New furniture. New books
piled on new floors.

The floor had to be new.
It broke beneath me
thirteen years ago.
A mist of dry
brown spores masked every
polished surface, choking
throat and lung until
one comic day
the whole thing just caved in.
"Dry Rot," they said.
Little is left for Memory
to hang on by,

and I don't ask or knock.
Why knock, why ask?
This different place contains
a different ghost
that stoops and scribbles
as if he were meant
more than the rest of us,
and more possessed,
inquiet, certain. He
lifts up his head.
I walk away through rain
to lose a past

I dare not say Goodbye to.
This last house
I lived in is, I see,
waste ground, stamped flat.
It hardly troubles me
more than to clutch
my raincoat closer.
Somewhere else has thought
Odysseus dead, that's all.
One Spring I moved
house, muse, life, love,
along here in a handcart.

A CHAIN OF DAISIES

At thirteen older than I,
her small coughs gently
pecking at daisies,
she was colt-legged Deirdre
breathy with laughters
round the lawn. She died,
the daisy petals tipped, then
blotched with red.

I cough now, a smoker's
cough: blue air
sags with tobacco
smoke, my chest
tightened by memory;
my heart pounds,
carrying weights of
serious middle age
up stairs into their
sagging married bed.

Those whom the Gods love
hide. I seek
through empty gardens where
her laughters hopped
and coughed that idle

summertime. My wife
eases her corset down,
heavy for bed.

And I can't tell her
what I think. It seems
ridiculous: a thin
flat-chested girl,
grassblades sticking to my
knees, crouched there
upon the balding
lawn, her chains
of daisies lengthening through
my smaller hands.

It sounds ridiculous;
and she, too, clowned,
laughed till her breath
gave out, then sat
fanning her yellow head
with dockleaves, crinkling
nose and eye to
ridicule my doubt.

She was so wise, and
coughed so much. The bed
sweats years of weariness
and love. I turn
for reassurance. Heart
bumps as we come
together, breathless
almost as this girl
arranging daisies in
my mind. I sleep
heavily, as God sleeps
who dreams us all.

AN ARRANGEMENT OF FLOWERS

Trapped by grief, we
nested upon a floor
of newspapers, the long days'
drinks gone sour,
our voices stumbling
round the past. It seemed
you'd bought disaster
blindly, as before
so many times, we both
so many times.

His paintings burned the
walls. Clumped flowers of ash
crusted and scabbed the light,
flaked silver tatters,
shone and quivered,
until thick air pressed
sobs from the frightened
lungs. He built and burned
nine years of ceremony
towards these flowers.

For those nine years of breath
his brushwork dragged
the cancerous radiance of
the eating rose
up through bones' trellis
from the belly's jar,
enduring blossoms.
Then he slowly died
under the taut smiles and
the swabbing hands.

You'd hated him for that,
for waste, for pain,
and for your pity;
ruthlessly alone
in your extreme survival
you betrayed
what nothing could betray,

threw parties, drank,
who other times bled nights
white as his flowers

or the papers' shaking
as we said
obituaries and shared a
death, your head
bent blonde and fearful
under loaded walls
that blossomed as your fingers
gripped and mourned
the loved, the hated,
undefeated dead.

CITY VARIETIES, LEEDS, 1963

The last time I drank here
I saw Tod Slaughter
play *The Demon Barber*.
He'd run back
between deaths
to the Circle Bar for gin.
Jenny was seventy then.
Was it five hundred
times, or over a thousand
he'd done her in?

His great long face
was flabby-white, his voice
a different resonant
century's, his head
magnificent. "I've always
played it straight.
You have to play these
grand things straight," he said.

We played ours almost straight,
but the run was shorter.
Once a year for three years
we played *Drink,
A Dripping Saga* through
the streets. I wore
a black top hat, moustache,
and cloak. They cheered,
hissed, laughed, and threw
tomatoes. We drank beer

and chased the girls.
Does that big blonde remember
my hand on her plump
bare tits beneath her mac,
walking back up Tonbridge
Street? And was it
that year the rotten fruit
finished off my cloak?

Dust dries my throat.
I have another Bass
on long dead lusts and
gaieties. No need
to burlesque their absurdities;
play them straight,
walking back from the bar
into the glow
of your nostalgia, enter,
gesture, wait,

and sound the heroic
statement. Love and Death
attend the slithering wigs
and wooden swords.
The Barber smiles. Time stops.
His razor lifts.
And from the Gods we
thunder daft applause.

In Cornwall

THE BALL
for Michael Seward Snow

Under the rock is an iron ball.
If you lie on your belly you'll see it there,
jammed between rock and rock at the top
of the roofed-in creek, so changed by air
and sea and age that its orange rust
burns like a sun. It is held fast where
rock roof meets rock. If you slither down
on a rope, he said, you can get quite near.

If you once get down, avoiding the pool
that is three foot deep, worn round by a stone
turning and turning upon the spool
of the spinning tide, and are big enough fool
to wedge your shoulders into that gap
you can touch the ball. It is rough with rust
and orange and ochre and red, he said,
a sun clamped down by a granite crust,

but you'll never move it. The sea is loud
as your heart as you lie on the slime and shift
your hand past your head chin on, the stone,
and every time that you try to lift
a muscle or twist the tide seems near
and the rock roof closer. The ball burns red
where roof meets rock: I hid it there
when I was a child of God, he said.

WEST PENWITH
for John Knight

These are the people of exodus.
Badger, seal, and gull
watch the dark faces and stiff hands
answer the journeying call.

Bells in the hollow cages
swing to the tide of night;

hymns from the granite chapels
drift through the emptied streets.

These are from Egypt, travelling
the bleak of the wide moor;
the badger's holt has tunnelled
under their histories' floor.

Stones in their moonshine circles
stare at the crossing hand;
shells of the tall mine buildings
shake at the west wind.

Silent and empty handed
the leader comes from Chun;
the seal's voice lifts across the stones
her undefeated tune.

Carns in their lonely ghosting
answer no one's hope;
over the harbour deep the gull
screams like a running rope.

These are the people of exodus;
moor and wave and wind
crowd round the white and squatting farms
and the west walls are blind.

CONSTRUCTION AND DIALOGUE
for Alexander Mackenzie

Construct a moor, a valley, and a sea.
Begin in that. We stand where these things are,
and speech is common, though the words erode
and wear away. Construct these steps, this room,
where we sit in our talk. Two have come here,
and two rub shoulders with the walking words.

I came here the hard way. In the cove
the stones are gods, hewn artifice of weather,
hacked-out women with slabbed breasts of rock,

men with bull jaws, rubbled beards, beasts
humped saurian on the sand to spit the sea.
Then I climbed the valley. Sweltering green
drenched the track between the bracken fronds,
and hawkbit flared. Queen Anne's lace nodded, mocked
in acid courtesy. The gorse buds blazed.
I climbed up the hard way. On the moor,
a mile from that first cove, and crouched above
this house earth falls away to, there were stones
threatening the search and journey, whale-white stones
bleached, scarred, waiting, huge upon the swell
and roll of the great deep. It is a country,
here, of falling darkness. Men are dragged
down through history, lashed in cruciform
upon the pocked and white flanks of the stone
as time is split to flinders. I came here
the only way there is to get here, talk
of where I've been as this is where we are
in venturing the small craft of a door
midway between the harbour and the moor.

And yet I trust no word of it. No phrase
will open up the somewhere we would go.
Speech is a common error. Talk runs clear,
and, secret in its strength as water, drags
and drowns obliquely. I say what I say
knowing a turned phrase may be heard and swerved
out of its quiet into rabbling foam
spun in the booming hollow of the rocks
or listened to like wind. I say 'I came'.
Whether or not that is the truth, who knows?

Now look out, across, down. Far below
a curvature of boats locked in a web
of their own making, verticals of masts
strung out with tensions where the piled-up town
slides down to stone hemmed in the lap of sea.
What will come of this? On iron rails
brown nets riddle the chill trembling light.
Each drift, this dusk, will gill its shoal of swimmers,
each cage crown rocked buoys where the wreckage spins.
It's not an answer. I look out, across.

The hill leans near, the grain of sky scraped clean
by wind honed off the rock, fields peeled of green
crumpled as leather, patched with linen snow,
and one house derelict. Who lives in there?
The cracked rind of its roof lies on black rooms,
and on one sill, smooth as an egg, a stone
rolled round from Iceland in a swerve of time.
See what we see from this place. Reassemble
syllables of listening. If we speak
we must arrange our echoing carries back
a language no words use, but all words hear.

Regard the moor, the valley, and the sea.
Begin in this. We talk where these things are,
and speech is common. You and I erode
and wear our words away as talking drags
its currents out beyond the harbour walls
below this room. Climb up to this word's room
and talk your journeys. Two are talking here,
and two rub shoulders with the walking words.

THE SLICKENSIDES

'Slickenslides' is a term used by geologists to refer to stones
which have been split by the movement of the earth's crust in
such a way as to form two polished surfaces facing one another.

'I sometimes think that stone,' he said,
'the slickensides, is just like us,
lying lonely in the dark,
two surfaces as smooth as glass

reflecting darkness, every smile
of meaning missed, each nod or wink
locked in the dark reflective heart',
and I replied, 'I sometimes think

two mirrors in the barber's room
reflecting I and I and I
are caused by just such fracture of
the cosmic unity.' His eye

brightened then. 'But *they* have light',
he said. 'The slickensides is blind.
You see yourself.' I saw myself,
a name continually signed

upon the darkness or the light
reflectively, no foreign chink
intruding me. I said, 'I'm blind. . . .'
And he replied, 'I sometimes think. . . . '

THE BLUE COAT
for Sylvia

The blue coat hangs
on the yellow wall.
The yellow wall
behind the blue
is made of stone.
The stone was laid
upon this hill
a world ago.

A world ago
upon this hill
men lived in stone
among the furze,
put up their walls;
the ring of stones
still holds the moor
above the house.

And in this house
are yellow walls.
Upon the wall
the coat is blue.
Should blue go out
upon the hill
this blue will walk
a world ago.

MAKING

for Ben Nicholson

It is not enough to be wise;
one must be lucky
with stone and wood and grass
and the taste of light
under the wall of the cottage;
one must listen,
as one breathes,
without selection or knowledge,
to the only shapes in the air
that make and echo
the one particular music.
One must turn
cleverly down the track
to the speaking sea
without disturbing the hills,
the patterns of footfall
light and heavy,
                heavy
and light,
        and light,
structuring the gradual
language that arrives
unspoken and complete
as a phrase of sparstone.

FROM THE ARTIST'S ROOF: ST. IVES 1956

for Ben Nicholson

Below the round and roof-swerve of the chapel
the blue and white
waters keep their counselling terms of boats;
ropes swing, with scoop and lift, their tethering message
to the walked walls, and the cross-hatch nets
lie like calligraphy on salts of stones.
From this roof over the town, a turning weather's
gold bird under us, the slipway roofs

edge slate light down across a hundred homes
to this statement, boats, like halcyons, curved
in planes and arms of walls as coarse as bread.
To stand here is to be a setting forth
and a returning; tethered as a bird
to the inscriptive planing of its wings,
we are acknowledgement upon its changing
into voyage or haven, and our words
lie across time like lines whose dip and lift
write testament upon all salt and bread
that we share here, while tumbler jug and plate
upon their commonplace extend the bounds
of every watched day's knowledge into acts
of lived discovery: the signs of light
and colour move like muscles from their stiff
and separation to a natural form
companionable and strange as love, and hold
the tense and slack of all ropes against light
and reach into the mind like tides. We stand
in this occasion, roofs and greys of shape
stretching to the undirected sea,
boats curved as worlds, and know we have come back
not into artifice, but to an air
that all inscription numbers with its minds,
and, in this air above the round and swerve
of the phrased chapel and the harboured terms,
light looks at us. Light is another sentence,
and we stand spelt here into breath and space.

THE COTTON DRESS
for Bonamy Dobrée

Love in a cotton dress.
No steadfastness
of star or Philomel
or thorn-spurred rose
red in the darkness,
but this happiness
walking as simply
as shadows down the road
no symphony attends

or lurking Troy.
It would be moving
if not commonplace,
such casual mastery
letting them dismiss,
as we dare not,
the dark, the loneliness.

THE NIGHT RIDE
for Michael Seward Snow

The road was black that Easter night;
ahead two eyes, eyes red as glass,
watched, then moved into the moor
to let our iron tumult pass.

Cold carved the face, hands held like death,
the broken moor slid roaring by,
and through the blind and narrowing walls
of villages and up the high

and final hill that Easter night
we saw two eyes, eyes red as glass,
that watched, then moved into the dark
to let our iron tumult pass.

AT THE CAVERN'S MOUTH: A DIALOGUE
for Alex and Pamela Currie

Once in the cave it was black as your hat.

No lights at all?
     I was blind with the shock.
I felt my way with nervous hands,
establishing contours of the wall —
humps big as hills, cracks deep as cracks
in the mind itself when a thing appals.

I carried a torch and the light came back
from the polished walls. I could see my way.

At first I was blind and for turning back.

But you didn't turn?

         I found the way.

It was easy, then?

         It was pretty tough.
Though I got to see the different degrees
of shadow and dark, and the way the rough
hewn faces stared in the lighter bits
and the hanging bats, I was pretty scared.

But you found the place?

         I found the place.

You were very moved?

         It was black as your hat.
I rested a while and thought aloud
and sang to keep my spirits up.

You didn't see . . . ?

         I didn't see
the crystal throne, the quartz like hands,
the coloured dome, the holy bone
fixed in the ice, or touch the bands
of silver round the central stone
they all report. I sat alone
in darkness there, and thought aloud,
and had a drink from the thermos top,
and heard the hollow echo as
I sang to keep my spirits up.

It was a failure, then?

         A flop.

You needed a torch. When I went down,
though I didn't go far, I could see it all;
the walls reflected back the light.

But you didn't go on?

              I was sure I would fall
in a pit or crevasse and I'd left it late
so I came away.

        You are going back?

Some day, some day when I have the time
and a guide as well.

          You will go alone.
There are no guides, and the booklet says,
for some reason or other, that only one
is allowed at a time.

          Was there much of a queue?
Not much. They mostly returned quite quick,
rather like kids who'd enjoyed The Wheel
tremendously, but looked rather sick;
they hadn't gone far.

         You took no light.
That seems so odd when you knew it was black
and you'd have to grope your way by the side.

I took a light, but the battery died —
I'm happy to say.

        Then it wasn't a flop?

It was failure all right, and that was the thing.
When you know you're blind and alone in the place
you think aloud and you start to sing,
and the echo tells you the hollow fact
that there is no image to tell the world,
no bright excuse for the easy air
of the travelled man.

But it's all been mapped —
photographed too!

              When I was there
it was something else. I sat alone.
I'd found the failure and could go back.

Any easy return?

              I knew the way.

There seemed more light?

              It was black as your hat.

THE ARRIVAL

         Listen. How long have you listened?
         Have you been listening long?
         I think I have been talking to you
         ever since the world began.

Who are you who come to the door?
Who are you who walk up this step
where the grass is dry
and the stone is cold
and the winter a terrible thing?

Who are you who come from the sea
with hands of waves and eyes of storms?
Who are you who climb from the sea
with the song of a gull
and the cry of a gull?

         I am a simple man come up
         from the long stoop of the sea.
         I have come a long way up the valley
         to ask your prayers for me.

I come from shores where ships find rock
and stave all timbers in.
I come from cities loud as birds
where money runs like gin.

I've come the whole world round about
to climb up from the sea
and walk up to your cottage door
and ask your prayers for me.

I've come from the turning weaving tide,
come from the long long wave
to ask you for your prayers for me
and ask for all you have.

I ask for everything you have,
for prayer is everything,
and as I knock upon the door,
Oh as I knock upon the door,
Oh as I knock upon your door
you'll hear the last bird sing.

But what is the bird that sings so loud?
What is the bird that answers the knock
when the sea is hushed
and the wind is hushed
and the summer a long ago thing?

Why do you come with your word from the sea
and a tale of waves and a talk of prayer?
Who are you who climb from the dark
with the gaze of a stone
and the smile of a stone?

Listen. How long have you listened?
Have you been listening long?
You know I have been talking to you
ever since your death began.

SANCREED CHURCHYARD

Wrestle, Jacob, with the stone angel,
and labour to give a fall to rock.
Across the moor the scythed striders
shoulder their grief. The widowed grass
round the humped marble withers tall.
The fool plays serpent on his panel.

The fool plays serpent on his panel.
The tower expounds that bells are tall
to shake their say. The sickled grass
falls to the elbows of the striders.
Even the gnat sings under the rock.
Wrestle, Jacob, with the stone, stone angel.

Wrestle, Jacob, with the quarried man,
the hewn and carted god, the cloud
that shaped the stone. The lonely striders
watch from the moor with all their grief.
The grass shakes out its flitting seed.
The serpent sings from the wood fool in his panel.

Don't tell me that the grave's a fine
and private place if you would stand
beside me here. Each name is worn
never so boldly as upon the stone.
This miller with his round mill stone
snores till the clappers have outworn
all history. Then he will upstand,
though all the worms have eaten fine.

Don't kid me that the whistling bird
pules for some dear and huddled bones,
or that the rank flowers sweating in their glass
are fed with tears from a lamenting boy.
This docked and dandelioned boy,
hid in his green hump, has a glass
of yellow rainwater. His bones
think less of grief than feathers of a bird.

Put by your monotones. These words
were live enough, and will come out
wearing their shames and trades to talk
your ordinary glories down.
That mossed cross may be fallen down,
that marble stained, but they will talk
how every weather kept tears out,
though all the mourners drowned in words.

I write these words for Hannah Kate.
Maybe she'll blink to show them true,
or maybe they will fall as flat
as trodden slate in the unlettered grass,
that open door that will not close
no matter what the locksmiths do.

I put this down because the corn
is burning flares of charlock out
as if to make somebody turn
here by the scratched and deadman stone
and think a triumph has been won,
though that's a long outdated thought.

Nevertheless, I write these words
for Hannah Kate has nought to do
but listen to the great unheard
verbs of the seasons from the hard
stone bolster of her easy bed,
careless of what is false or true.

Sans creed, I walk the crowds of stones,
rub shoulderbones below the tower
with summaries of praise and grief,
and gravely ask the spinning worms
what backchat, drunk with stars and owls,
allows the day of time to pass
for these, hobnobbing with slate words
from cold doorways in the grass.

Spineless as strawberries, they nod
beneath the rank green havoc grown
across the quiet words I spell
to Glory, Mercy, Peace, and God,
pretending sleep. They will not hear
no matter what great text you drop,
but, dead as mutton, deaf as posts,
continue spitting daisies up.

It's a great life the dead have here.
The bullyragging sun's shut out,
the drifting thistle-clocks keep time
with every skull's most private thought,
and insolent as sudden rain
their quiet mocks the leaning stones,
safe in the peace of our unrest
who pay taxes to cold bones.

Wrestle, Jacob, with the stone angel
that wears his mockery for grief.
Upon the moor the weathered preacher
fingers his stops. The granite dancers
stiffen to wind across the fields.
The serpent plays the fool upon his panel.

The serpent plays the fool upon his panel.
The hammered bells announce the fields
are green to sing. The gathering dancers
lassoo the stiff text of the preacher.
The chiselled words erode their grief.
Wrestle, Jacob, with the tall, tall angel.

Wrestle, Jacob, with the lifting man,
the given prison-breaker, born
to carve on stone. The lonely preacher
sings from the moor his waking grief.
The grass dries in a storm of seed.
The wise fool steps with serpent from his panel.

For The Muse

THE REQUEST

You, Who exist
as the place where head, heart, limbs,
become their unity
to move in love

towards the understanding
acts of God,
possessing and possessed
by humandkind,

do not condemn, but
salve the wounds received
in alien service under
cheating banners,

and bring reverence on such
armoured ranks
as fought unblessed
and were by dreams betrayed.

INVOCATION

Be with me, Muse; I need the dream
of loveliness, as all men must
who see the phantom of the flower
blossom in the mindless dust,

and in that moment's gasp recall,
or think that they recall, an hour
impermeable to stain and rust,
a quenchless flame, a soaring tower,

a nakedness as of a girl
who is the nakedness she shares,
and is most near, however far,
and bears the moon and wears the stars.

ONE WORD

One word from her
and I am trapped again,
snared by the dazing
perfume of her hair,
bewildered by her breasts,
her thighs, her lips,
again love's victim
and lust's prisoner,

gasping, ridiculous,
a landed fish
flapping beneath her lifted
golden rod,
a cenobite confounded
in his cell
by entry of the radiant
flesh-kissed god.

THE ARRIVAL

You entered upon the company
like a flame,
red-gold hair burnished,
amber velvet gown
flowing to moving thigh
and mounded breast,
green eyes alight,
skin white as thistledown,

yet seemed astonished
at the sudden pause
in conversation
and the startled eyes
of those who'd thought you
no more than a girl
and had not guessed
your lien on Paradise

nor understood
what now they understand,
seeing you loose your beauty
and its powers
upon the casual evening
as a Queen
once loosed her splendour
to the Trojan towers.

FLAMEN

As you came naked
through my door
my heart gave such a
sudden leap
I had no power
to do more
than gasp to see
that phantom shape

of love's desire
at last made flesh,
at last made incarnate
for my praise;
you paused a moment,
half ashamed,
half proud of my
astonished gaze,

then, smiling in your
cowl of hair,
simplicity and
candour came
to burn your body
on my own
and sanctify us
in the flame.

TWO MORALITIES AND A FOOTNOTE

I

In a shop advertised as selling "Aids
to Better Vision" (scorning the low term "glasses") ,
the portrait, horn-rimmed, of a poet looks down
on all the myopoeia that passes,
thinking of something else, no doubt, but not
(I dare assume) the symbolism of sight —
more probably how that one's hair is gold
and this one's skirt deliriously tight.

II

Last night we played the animal. Today
I hear you singing to the children. "There,"
I think, "she goes !" It seems I muscled in
on private tunes which, glad to have me share,
you now make free confession of; our feet
were mingled to that sweet barbaric air.

And yet tonight I'll greet, man being brute,
eyes not quite virginal, though make-up chic,
smart shoes, smart handbag, and conspiring grin
boasting the curly fleece this Jason seeks
with hardening muscle, and, as we begin,
will hear the same tune hissing through her teeth.

III

You condemn this Muse, but yet, observe,
it was Her finger on the climbing nerve
that played the tune old blinded Homer wrote
of History with its mouth on Helen's throat.

THE WHISPER

This poem for her
moves slowly
into the room,
its dazed head
troubled with beauty,
its slow tongue
mumbling of awe
at a girl heard
saying *Write me
a poem*, meaning
only *Be busy!*
but with her sly
assertive body
murmuring *Show me
now the Muse
you say I am.*

THE PRESENCE

I do not know
her look, her smile,
her dress, her name,
but only while

I make my poems
that there is she
within the darkness
facing me.

QUATERNION

I

Seeing Her in Her various disguises,
broad wife, black-sheathed schoolgirl, swinging tart,
blonde, brown, lissom, squabby, moist-eyed, dozy,

how can he tell realities apart
enough to know which one will fit his crown
and drag across the stage Her blinding curtain?
Only the unsought, unthought, strange-eyed bitch
will plague that itch and make his verses certain.

II

Offend Her, if you must, with random women,
drink, drugs, thievery, or lay nations waste —
these She may tolerate as venial, but
once boast of cunning or inflate your taste
into a principle of separate rule,
you'll feel the downturn of that sovereign hand,
and, old or young, cold scholar or hot fool,
will tumble, gaunt and wordy, with the damned.

III

This man who is dead made poems.
                                Now on his grave
I scatter public leaves, gloss-darkened holly,
spotted laurel, blue-green ferns of yew,
woven into a hubless, spokeless, holy
wheel — the usual dismissive token
of the turning year, and of completion.

But the Angel sorrowing above stone
in stone humility his heirs provide
I give no leaf to; she leans, gravely dressed
in robes and misery, who should bestride
this huddle, arms akimbo, out-thrust hips,
bared breasts, wild hair, triumphant parted lips.

IV

Wrestle this Angel, and whoever falls
to head-lock, arm-lock, hip-tilt, threshing thigh,
it is Her victory, or none at all.

Hers is that last, wild, conquering, plundered cry.

NINE FOR THE MUSE

I

Darkness remembers . . .
Through the dark a face
formed, fleshed bronze,
a woman. It was Her
again, Her mouth moving.

Back to mind it comes.
I sweat, tremble,
suddenly seeing Her clear,
my heart bumping

at an encounter
in this inadequate place
where everything, an act
of evasion, stammers
lying intimacies
or embarrassing histories
of absurdity,
Her substitutions,
hungry, eyes closed, breathless,
stains of dampness
in the heat of the bed,
and salt sweat drying
stale in the roots of
tossed hair.
        Then at night
through dark again Her face
fleshed bronze, the moving
mouth, the syllables
muscular with silence
gathering and knotting
words which must be unheard
always, and always known. . . .
I sit in daylight
watching the memory form,
dissolve, my fingers
fumbling the knots in thc air,
untying, tying.

II

Part of the need
is like animals to nuzzle
warmly, wetly,
in the dark of the car
rolling the buildings backwards,
the night streets backwards,
to eat the smells and the softness,
to fondle and curl
together and fumble mysterious,
being mysterious
together and roughly and gently —
not two persons
but two mammals
moving in warmth and softness,
two kissing tongues,
and the all-encompassing Presence
gathering, nearing, sharing —
but part of the need
is, unlike animals,
to say "No", say "Maybe",
drawing back from the ultimate
brink of the will
to part on a doorstep
cherishing minute pain.

III

Suddenly, light!
There was a girl in rain,
rain wet upon her cold face, infinite tears
of candour upon our passion,
our pressing mouths.

Beauty has no deceptions.
Final light
reduces nothing, counters
nothing so
transfixed by purity.
A young, young girl,
rain on her face,
and I poised for the journey

out and unknown continents,
her eyes
blue, cornflower blue,
her new breasts round and firm,
her blonde hair soft. . . .
I have not been deceived.
Parting and silence
merely are a pause
between realities.
Again it strikes!
She walks my youth towards me
through the rain.

IV

Love is eternal but not
endless,
            fades,
fails, dwindles, shatters.
Once an eye, a gaze
that men went mad for;
then a plaster myth
leant in a corner
among dust and flies.

In proper reverence
we make our vows
lifelong and break them,
tremble to the snare,
willing and breathless,
and yet all we steal
is always given
long before we stir
and by the hands
we think we rob,
                for Love
has part in every kiss,
keeps every bed,
indifferent to moralities
or lies,
and blesses common lust
with sudden good
and friendship with
destructive Paradise.

V

In Venice once, a girl —
I invent nothing —
leaning on her elbow,
naked, above me,
thinking that I was asleep,
caressed
the twin buds of her breasts
as if her hand
contained the myriad children
we had spilled
between us in the casual
passionate bed,
and, mothering, whispered
something in a tongue
less than Venetian
or much more, the words
triumphant, salutory.
Then, as arms
reached up to pull her down to me,
she chilled
and almost cried:
if I had come from sleep,
I would have seen her
in a mask of gold
and without breath,
yet speaking without breath.
We clung surprised
into indefinite selves.

VI

Everywhere it happens,
here and everywhere.

It may be this girl, or this,
the uncountable Muse

clad in conviction
for whatever moments,

marriages, cities, bedrooms
can survive

our desolate introspection
and inform

the blind encounter
with Her changeless word.

It could be today, tomorrow.
There is no end

of sudden manifestation,
variant hope,

glimpsed, it may be, for seconds,
or, as now,

held in the mind over distance,
memory brooding.

VII

Astonishment commands
the centuries;
                      there
in the Uffizzi,
beckoned by a smile,
they swerved and buckled :
I was face to face
with my own heartbeat;
though four hundred years
had shared the canvas,
yet it was her smile
and my own memory:
I could recall
the softness of the mouth,
the scent of breasts,
distinctly — more distinctly
than so much.

It pierces, this.
It pierces and transcends.

Or should I say it answers?
I have spent
more times than these
upon more shores than these,
and memories of loves
are what survive
the subterfuges
of our deaths.
                We wake
from blindness rarely,
rarely see the shape
that pierces time
and ruins space and law,
and then it is with Her,
or Her, or Her,
and lasts the endless
minute of a kiss.

VIII

This is dangerous.
I am approaching danger;
a girl in a long black coat,
blonde falling hair,
and a smile that is memory,
she comes
out of the future and past.
The present is pain
always, the split in the husk
a long deep pain,
the wings uncrumpling an agony.
What is dreamed
may be only a dream,
but what avers
its presence to the waking mind
entranced
into foreknowledge
cannot be denied
one step towards perfection.
I am afraid,
yet dare not pray for escape
from the face of praying,
or from Her wish

that She has made my wish,
but only trouble my heart
with a plea for protection.

IX

Memory moves through the figments
seeking love,
but suddenly, through dark,
fleshed bronze, a face
forms again in the stillness.
I extend
my arms, head lifted, strain my throat
to speak
Her ventriloquial messages,
Her welcome,
and Her call for courage,
but sweat slips
the stone away, between my
clutching hands,
and I am small below
that cold colossus
intellect piles on pavements
of the will
to block out nature.
I am lost, thrown down.
Slaves jeer and gather.
Then, through dark, a face,
bronze into flesh,
the mother of my children,
the woman of my bed,
the warmth and stir
of lust and gratitude.
The vision moves
through figments and through memory
granting love
to every commonplace;
we mingle hands
and feel Her watching
from where histories end.

Happenings

THE HAPPENING

Surely it is about to happen again.
The field is brown with summer; the small clouds
waste away in wisps; the sea is steady:
everything is ready for its return.

I approach the likelihood with a sense
of glad anxiety; it could bring the same
sudden pull of muscle, the same unbalance
into the quickening rage, the compulsive chance,

or prove dangerous. I have never known
it leave me stilled so long. Maybe it wakes
gradually in some rank forgotten corner,
lifting its head from rags, to mouth and groan

luxuriously before it stretches, tenses
to my supine muscle, pads across
the necessary silence, coils and leaps.
I dared not lay myself to sleep unless

I knew it waiting. Already I find it hard.
The air is thick. The summer has lived so long
it wastes away like grass. The sea is steady.
Always I am unready, unprepared,

deliberately at ease. Will it never happen,
never happen again? I scratch my scars,
walking into the morning, undiscovered,
unassailed, grown desolate with mercies.

WINTER SCENE

The street is done in greys and browns;
the careless brushwork of the snow
lets perceive blank canvas through
the drab scene we have learned to know

from constant use as background for
our grave, absurd emergencies.
In the foreground, creatures, black
and dazed as smoke, surprise our eyes

recognizing here are we
scurrying on our usual tasks
disquietedly. But where we go
the painter does not know, and asks

his question of the brown facades,
the grey trees' quivering skeletons:
behind our world are all things blank?
What business are we out upon?

The composition needs us here
as foreground to time's wintry sense,
but is our darkness, more than snow,
a passing flurry of pretence?

THE SHELL

Find a sea shell on the shore;
hold it in your calloused hand;
hear the surging roar on roar,
hear the crumbling of the land;
see the silent suck and slow
insistent pawing clay and rock,
dark tidal murmurings below
each superficial wreck and shock.
Then pull the nail from hulk of wood
black beneath the coble's rust;
drive that nail into the shell,
watch phoenix-like from osseous dust
the red rose grow and bud and bloom,
let fall its fruit upon the sand.
Split it open. Find a shell,
and hold it in your calloused hand.

ELEGY FOR DEAD SPLENDOUR

'Everyone knew about her jewels, her monogrammed initials and
her visiting cards, which bore only the words, "Mrs. Vanderbilt".
She died in seclusion in a curtained room.'

The Yorkshire Post, January 1953.

I

This year's beginning, a dead age
gropes memory with its parrot claws;
the stiffened Ruritanian cloak
lies crumpled on the centuries' floor.

Cold as cold pearls are her eyes;
about her neck the stones are chilled:
did she offend, to be so decked,
against that lonely Nashville child,

that debutante whose life eloped
with its romance to learn control,
manipulate the mannered strings
of pageants in a limelit world,

whose gestures masked ironic pride
that found regality a doom,
condemned to grow a woman old
secluded in a curtained room?

II

Hers were the gems of human need;
the vivid garnet on her hand,
deep as a wound, reflected nights
the opal of her dreams had stained;

her diamonds, splintered from the light,
inscribed each mirror with deceit;
the bright spurred coral at her breast
cried exile from the sounding seas,

and sapphires, empty as her skies
of childhood, starred the air with frost:
no robbery could broach her hoard,
no broker estimate the cost,

but, in the gold-clawed basilisk
upon her ruling hand, she saw
the crowned heads crowding round her throne,
the era welcome them, then fall.

III

This year's beginning, Kings and Queens
pack memory in their suited state;
Hohenzollern, Bourbon, Guelf,
dealt her pageantry of fate,

for carnival's Kingfisher plumes
masked a wounded nakedness.
No hero came but, wasting, fell
into the luxury of success;

need petrified, desire's eyes
suffered an alchemic change;
her pearls retain the shape of tears,
her diamonds the gall of chains,

her dark our grail; Romance's Kings
fade perilous before her tomb:
the quest is dead; an age has died
secluded in a curtained room.

NIGHT PIECE

Darkness, comfortable with strangeness,
answers the loud breath on the road
between trees, slides hands
together, gives its creatures good

of warmth, of nearness, tricks distance.
Midnight, indiscreet with cars,
blazes, passes. Time dwindles
into a false hypothesis.

This I remember, but can not
manoeuvre back. With you, alone
by small hedgerows, it seems darkness
belongs to lovers and to children.

We are no longer native; wish
hard as we may, we cannot earn
the infinite space between dusks,
the innocent independent kingdom

of doubt, admission, fervour, shame.
We grope back to the waiting car,
turn the key, accuse our age
with a sick animal's defenceless roar.

A BALLAD OF DESPAIR

Mercy, Pity, Peace, and Love.
    I met a walking man.
He walked each street towards despair
    and stared up at the sun.

This way he walked. A sawdust head
    knocked on his coughing chest.
A hand twitched like an empty glove.
    A boot scratched at the dust.

That way he was. He was that way.
    Flame throbbed within his head.
The wax mouths of his five children
    spoke like they were dead.

'The Lamb that died' the preacher said.
    He saw the Lamb that died.
There was a black cloud round its head,
    a law book at its side.

'Love your neighbour', said the preacher,
    'and obey the Law.'
He saw the blinded fishermen
    die on the green shore.

He saw his brother spitting sand
    with barbed wire round his head.
His hands like rags turned his door key.
    His mouth shone like lead.

He climbed the stair. At the first step
    He saw a city burn.
Children with flesh like trailing rags
    watched him from the turn.

The second step he took, the sea
    delivered up its dead.
The shoals of miles shone their white bellies
    at his staring head.

And the third step he climbed, he stopped.
    He stood stiff as a door.
A thousand blinded tongueless creatures
    coupled on the floor.

He stopped, then climbed. He went into
    the room his children lay.
He knew that he was mad as truth
    to take their lives away.

He knew that truth was mad. He walked
    the darkness of the street,
cried, 'Suffer the little children
    to die in a clean sheet.'

He climbed the headline steps outside
    the black industrial hall,
cried, 'Though the children ask for bread,
    what bread is there not stone?'

What bread not stone? I met him dressed
    in pity and in blood.

I met him knelt in Calvary Place
      beside his children's bed.

Mercy, Pity, Peace, and Love,
      I saw him lift his gun.
He lay like logic in the street
      and stared at the blind sun.

HOUSE AND SCHOLAR
for Tony Connor

He thought of buying this old house,
in love with stone-flagged floors,
beams that retained the twist of the tree,
and a landscape melted by thick windows.

He pondered on the leisureliness of time
transforming time, conceiving monumental
order grown from ordinary lives,
their day-in and day-out renamed "traditional."

Something here had kept a kind of faith.
Taking a turn about the unkempt garden
(green pelt upon millpond, quince in orchard,
moss hillocked on the mounting block, earth sodden) ,

he felt that living here might be a way
of owning history, making no departure
from the long dead, answering their names
in their own language from an ignorant future.

Ghosts were half his mind. He had been talking
ghosts up now for what seemed like forever,
sipping his blood into their mouths. He picked
seeds from dead grass and told them like a lover.

But the house said nothing. Nothing spoke.
A nearing car replaced it in the past.
He watched a fringe of rain bead swollen eaves,
and all he could remember was the cost.

GOOD TIME GIRL

The girl was young. He whispered to his mate
he'd lay her and then chuck her from the car.
Her breasts were small. Her legs were thin and crossed.
She swung a pointed shoe as at the bar
he slopped two coffees, carried them, sat down.
He had no doubt she'd let him get that far.

Not long from school most probably. I heard
her saying that he talked 'a lot of cock'.
She was relaxed and equable. She knew
it was expected, felt no sense of shock.
This wasn't the first time she'd let a boy
do that with her. Her hand was firm as rock

as she picked up her cup. Ten minutes more
they chatted idly, casually, smiled
without much interest, and then got up
and went outside for her to be defiled.
A commonplace occurrence. She had known
the pattern of it since she was a child.

The pick-up in the Caff. The ride. The act.
The after-cigarette. The cool good-night.
The only thing she'd get to show was sex;
that's all they like her for. If she'll put out,
who cares about the rest? Who ever cares?
She has good times.
                    And hasn't she the right?

MAN WITH NEWSPAPER

The man in the corner with the nervous tic
lifting the rim of his lip to show a tooth
as yellow as the cake crumbs on his plate,
observes in silence the immaculate Truth
of half an evening paper which he shakes
tenderly as he reads of sinful youth

as if this delicate shaking could dislodge
a section of the print, which, like a cliff,
would slide down to the sea and so lay bare
a whiter taller cliff, almost as if
he knew instinctively what he'd see there
when that black evening surface had sloughed off,

and, undeterred by failure, must go on,
assured of something no one else could find —
words wriggle down the page, and colons roll
like pebbles, and the headlines, undermined,
split off and slither down towards the crash —
land in his lap, perhaps, — but never mind,

it would be worth the bruises, broken cups,
and shattered dirty plates, if he could tell
what lay behind. His lip jerks in a flick
of horse-lip as at sugar it can smell
but thinks delusory, and all around
his table conversations rise and swell

unnoticed but for one glad secret peep
at these he will astonish. His green eye
is haunting as a mirror two rooms deep,
and probing as a fish. A lazy fly
drowns in the cup that no one has removed,
and passing aircraft tremble through the sky.

SPILT COFFEE

Yes, she is sure. It's three weeks late.
Spilt coffee makes a sluggish pool
for fingers to trace out their past
and lose the future. He's a fool.
Of course she knows. How could she not?
Her eyes are questioning and cool

as they glance up from underneath
the mop of bright transfigured hair
she's hung above the coffee pool

her brooding guides. She has sat there
above the pool for half an hour.
Pools don't get you anywhere.

And that's a comfort. She is done.
Life's caught her out. And why resist?
She tried some pills but just got sick.
Her other hand trapped in his fist
knows that she'll always wonder at
what she was aiming when she missed.

PUBLIC HOUSE DOMINOES

And down they clack. Four pairs of hands
in puddling shuffle. Take them up.
Who's got the sixes? Fire away!
They slap them on the table top
as if each number was a chance
of making Heaven blow its top!

They play like curses. Number one,
the nearest to the window, looks
as if he runs a little shop
for rubber goods and dirty books;
it's how his mouth looks when he talks,
and how he giggles when he blocks.

And number two that's leaning back?
I'd say a disappointed man.
His whiskers droop like ginger weeds,
and his nose and eyes both run.
He's blocked again. Another knock.
Why does he bother to go on?

But number three . . . Still rather young.
I'd say he's something of a lad.
He plays it cool and doesn't care.
If I'd had all the birds he's had
I wouldn't mind. That wavy hair
is not the stuff he got from Dad!

I wonder why they let old Four
in on the game. He's knocking on.
Someone's Grandad, I expect.
He's gone and got the numbers wrong.
That's the fourth time he's tried to match
a two against a double one.

They're a right bunch to take to games!
I can't think why they have to live.
Except of course, to pick a three
or five or eight or six, and give
the table that tremendous clout.
And yet they never play it out.

A MAN WATCHING

Girls in black leather touch his heart;
even the blurred lips of the young
that pout beneath huge helms of hair
suggest a paradise to come

so long as down the little backs
a stiff and supple leather creaks
its slanting shine, or gleaming black
and upturned collars, cupping cheeks

and heavily emphatic eyes,
assert their chill destructive gloss;
the thin bird-voices twitter as
he reverently explores his loss,

a tongue that touches on a gap;
his thought grows turgid hot and thick;
they leave the Caff; the engines roar;
within his heart a beast lies sick.

A BALLAD OF JOHNNIE QUESTION
for John McDonald

This for Johnnie Question
    who made man his mark,
travelled the live rails of his bone
    along the tunnelled dark.

This verse for his thin-boned wrist,
    for his two threadbare rooms,
the rented stair and the sour gaslight
    and the yellowstone.

And this verse for the Wanted Ads,
    the forms, the dotted lines,
the echoing Assistance Board,
    and for the wind and rain.

This for the wind and for the rain.
    He pocketed his pride,
knocked it against his only shilling
    at his manhood's side.

And for his manhood, this. He took
    his everywhere to heart,
rapped iron on the every wooden
    door that locked him out.

And the first answer said to him,
    'Responsibility.
You took your own life on your head.
    What must be, must be.

Accept and work.' He turned aside.
    Upon the sooty stone
he saw the words, 'God so loved man
    that man must love alone.'

And the second answer was,
    'The wisdom of the State
demands mobility of labour,
    and a reasonable Rate.

Learn proportion.' He turned back.
          Upon the civic wall
he saw the words, 'God so loved man
          no man need love at all.'

O who was Johnnie Question
          that was meek and shy,
walking the bare streets of his bones
          with a staring eye?

This verse for his half of bitter,
          for his leaking shoe,
the girl that bore his white children,
          and for the football queue.

And this verse for the pin-up
          and for the public name,
the statesmen and the bulletin,
          and this for the wind and rain.

This for the wind and for the rain,
          and for his manhood this.
He knocked upon the door of all
          the old eternities.

The answer came. 'To give to all
          that asked would ruin all.'
He watched the ruined poster flap
          upon the churchyard wall.

The answer came. 'The Charities
          and State may help you out.'
O, who was Johnnie Question
          to make the faithful doubt?

O, who was Johnnie Question?
          What did he learn at school?
Upon the blackboard, 'God is Love,
          Expediency, and Rule.'

This verse for the answerers,
          and for the rich man's gate,
the Economist, the Politician,

and for the Church and State.
And this for Johnnie Question,
        for his manhood shame,
the shilling knocking at his thigh,
        and this for the wind and rain.

THE STREET
for Tony Connor

Lost in the ordinary street, he turned
and stared up at the ordinary blinds,
and knocked, half-hearted, at a peeling door,
not that he thought he'd learn from the reply,
or even that he'd know to tell them why
he'd come this way, or what his walk was for.

No one replied or stirred. Nothing was changed.
No echo boomed. No shuffling slipper made
its apprehensive pause before the latch.
They'd gone away. He'd known before he knocked
the house was certain to be double locked,
and anyway all answers have a catch.

Lost in the ordinary pause before
the locked and peeling ordinary door,
he knew he'd meet no one the least surprised.
This was a common spectre of the street,
the broken shoes upon the aimless feet,
the absence, and the question, and the lies.

It wasn't that they didn't care to get
strangers or answers in the street, and yet
it wasn't accident the blinds were down.
Something had gone away. He could stay lost,
or telephone the police and ask the cost
of questioning every suspect in the town.

GUIDE BOOK

You'll need a guide. This Baedaker of the back
alleys and cul-de-sacs of the old town
everyone gets lost in, except the lost
who have given up thinking they know their way around,
has been compiled from evidence supplied
by those we trust; inform us if they lied.

Some inexactitudes of course occur.
The price of a bed can vary day to day,
and though our minimum estimate is reliable
the maximum can be much more than we say,
more perhaps than you have, which is a pity
if you are alone and friendless in the city.

Still further advice, well-tested and well-tried:
Don't drink the water if you want to live
without discomfort. It may seem cold, clear,
sparkling, revitalising, but can give
a thirst which is unquenchable, a thirst
which of all possible fevers is the worst,

incurable, I'm afraid — or nearly so.
Sometimes it's intermittent. Sometimes age
weakens the intensity of the attacks.
Their seriousness is difficult to gauge.
The natives show their famous wit in giving
the stuff a nickname which means (roughly) Living.

Other food aspects: Do try Bouillabaise!
Delicious! All the fish-wealth of the sea
is used to make it. You may find it rich,
with curious tastes and strange anatomy,
but don't be put off. An acquired taste,
which, once acquired, never goes to waste.

Fish is, indeed, their forte in these parts.
They say the girls have fish-scales on their thighs,
and there's a story that a King Crab takes
each summer the most beautiful as prize;
quaint stories told now less as superstitions
than as a jibe at regional conditions.

To sum up, then: Fish yes, but Water no !
It almost seems a paradox. They say
bathe in the ocean after eating fish
and a great dolphin carries you away
through life, through death, and so much else beside,
or so we hear; inform us if they lied.

THE EXPLORATION

I walked into the mountain heart.
The corridors were choked with dirt,
the roof decaying. Rubbled stone
blocked the great gate of the room,
and the huge bones of animals,
long extinct, lay where they fell
below a gap of ragged light
becoming grey. It was too late
to pass the broken and the spilled
and venture on the room by night,
alone and sure that I would find
the dancing frescoes figured round
a central cold, a hollow place.
No man, alone, could lift his face
and stare upon them without dread
and understanding of the dead
shaking him until he bowed.
I turned back and my heart was loud
to hide from me in upper air
the secret running of the deer,
but all the walls of looming night
were figured with their wheeling bright
and breaking forms, and in each tread
I stumbled home those hunters bled,
those hunters dead. I could not sleep.
No images were mine to keep.
Man on his cross dies many times
and many times the mountains weep.

THE GAME

He answered pools with pebbles where the sun
hung in its blue void between paving stones,
took aim and shattered it; a liquid ridge
of broken stars leapt into space and ran
with shock on shock out almost to the edge
his feet pinned down, then wavered and was gone.
The sun still hung there. He would stand and wait
till it was hard and firm as his two feet,
then bend and scrabble and take aim again.

I stood and watched him answering one pool
all afternoon. I'd thought that it might pall
and he shrug off the game, but it went on,
stone upon stone, as if he kept a rule,
persistently compelled. Above, the sun
hung like a stranger, empty and unreal,
the sky remote. Between his earth-fixed feet
it seemed there hung some question he must meet.
I saw my own sun in another pool.

ROBERT GRAVES, A SNAPSHOT

At sixty-four in the family swing,
standing straight, neither grave nor fooling,

hands on the twin ropes in a slack grip,
mouth still, eyes watchful, head gone grey on top:

pride, you might think it, in his young mind
or long-tested carpentry, then, at a bound,

leap into metaphor, that alternation,
(earth, sky, earth) child's wild risk, poet's profession.

AN UNFORTUNATE INCIDENT

Having built the maze of words, stones, trees,
(Instructive and Entertaining) who is it comes
paying admission but a sea-stained gentleman
with yards of knitting wool tied to his thumbs?

Perhaps he'll retrace his steps when he sees the children
(In Charge Of Adults) , the youths and the giggling girls.
But, No ! He smiles with quiet confidence,
limps through the wicket and starts to pay out his wool.

I would not for the world have let this happen.
Already the lovers' seat at the centre has changed
and the children are growing frightened. Even the adults
are talking of getting back for the tea and scones.

It's too late now to think of refusing him entry.
(The Management Reserves the Right, of course.) He's
          found
the trick of that final turning. Something is waiting.
It isn't at all the sort of thing I'd planned.

My little problem once had a quite different answer —
a small lawn, a seat for the lovers, — but *he* had to come
and go (as I see he is doing now, composedly)
winding the yards of red wool back on his thumbs.

TWO INCIDENTS FROM *THE VOYAGE OF THE BEAGLE*
for Geoffrey and Margaret Keynes

I   THE GENERAL

Music he asked of that grave general,
and, put aside,
considered in his mad mind, asked again,
and met again the same unkind reversal,

and then the third time ventured, heard the laugh.
The fool ran, ran,
but the brute soldiery ensnared him, half
innocent, half singing man,
and pegged him out like hide beneath the sun.

Afterwards he said, 'If you should hear
that laugh resound,
know there's no pity; silly man or sound
must recognize the echoing hounds of fear
released upon him without stay or stop.
Though he may run,
the sentence stands and he must drink that cup,
half animal, half carrion,
must burn out blame to the symphonic sun.'

II.   THE DARK ENCOUNTER

That day the barren island swooped like a gull
upon, then away from, the boat as we swore and pulled
through the rocks that were oily with sea-sweat
and warted with shells
to the blank shore crumpled with weathers
and hauled her over
the shingle and camped by the cliff in a midnight of squalls;

the next day they left their forest, jostling, a herd
of sniffing and itching and clicking and staring hard,
and they shuffled up close to our boat side,
then, growing unawed,
they were daft loud laughter all over
and quick as fever
to mimic like mirrors our every gesture and word,

reflecting back our vision, learning to grope
in harshness for laughter, in grimace for smile or gape,
and at last we perceived there, distorted,
the dark of our scope,
and were bored black sick with the business
and started to curse.
We stayed there a week, exploring, but left without hope.

NURSERY WALLPAPER

Tom, Tom, brass in a woodwind landscape,
stole a pig, in his rebellion
gold against blue trees and cushats calling,
one with the cymbal sun. And after sleep
children awake to watch his red-capped running
along an unheard wall, and his escape,
always at climax, chuckled through new hands
fumbling their own design against love's cooing.

But there is also Mary, cool as cream,
planting the scallops' quiet by red flowers,
bells tinkling as Christ-cake with its wondering white
and tapers tall as sleep. And after dreams
young hands place counters round, design the rite
of life's perfection on the wood-block's gleam,
and mimic her neat plot upon the wall
that fades, irradiant in morning light.

Morning moves round; lit square on paper square,
the figures shine in patterning to the mind
each possible significance of shape
and action round the moment. Topless towers,
walls of bricks or letters, after sleep
are in the wall's world, maid and shell and flower
risen up from rhyme, contrary bells
to Tom, still running in his ritual landscape.

DISCOVERY
for Jacob Kramer

The stones were round where he picked them,
and the shells sharp-edged,
the tide a slip of lace far out across the sands,
golden as youth in the summer by the cote d'azur,
and hard as the thighs of young girls running,
dancing, and laughing in sunlight before their shadows.

The time was noon when he picked them,
and the sky clear,

the mountain a purple mystery across the meadows,
vague as the words before sleep in the arms of lovers,
and calm as the eyes of young boys waking,
silent and empty to sunlight upon their faces,
the future cool as a pigeon's egg and smooth,
the time to come as graceful as the turn
of gull down sand dunes, and the morning rounded
in its promise as a pigeon's egg.

Where he found them the pools were deep
and the rock
crimson and green with weed, and silvered by snails,
and veined with ochre, and round;
and the pools were dark,
where the wide-lipped wounds of anemones
silently ached,
and the hesitant claw of the hermit
wrinkled the sand,
and the small unknowing minnows moved like notes
of music through the wires of drifting tendrils:

and as he stooped before the world of waters,
hollowed in rock, as close curved in the palm
of noonday as the penny of a child
gazing with fearful awe at the Future's entrance
and the tall doorman with the sand moustache
and eyes of sky in thunder,
suddenly
the shapes came into focus and he saw them,
defined in their several ways by the stillness
for the first time,
and above the round stones where he picked them
the sun was highest,
and all his years smooth and deep as pools.

HALCYONE

Girl to feathers over the death-spumed sea:
seven days of the year the winds pause,
a nest of black twigs swinging her births of tides,
his broad wings stiff above her like a cross.

This, written in a dead tongue, handed down
household to household as the nations fell
and rose again and princes washed their hands
in stone rooms walled against the wrack and swell,

moves yet — the casual ordinary girl,
the death at sea, the white corpse dragging home
its wreaths of weed and wheeling gulls, the hush
of shingle shirring in the very bone,

bringing a miracle. As we, too, mourn
the drowned of days and faces and bend down
to see what must be seen, something is changed,
and, if we do not shiver into wings

across all ways and days, it is but time
that, grown despicable and covetous,
allows no grief its own, though through all years
the black twigs swing beneath the wing and cross.

THE NET
for Samuel Banks

The blue day was an apple in the hand
when she came smiling to his boyish wars;
the aeons were early and the gods were young.
No matter how you watch from where you stand
or if you doubt or symbolise the cause,
she smiled upon him and the smiles were young.

Time has no way of passing when we wake
to implications of the eyes and stance,
the blue day's ever in a grain of sand,

the fall impossible. We see them take
their places in the shaking breathless dance.
The aeons were early and the time was once.

But always lame and clever someone comes
and round the simple day the bright net falls.
They found their nakedness had been surprised.
She purified herself in Paphian foam
and he went cold and wise back to his wars.

KING AND QUEEN
for Henry Moore

The big hands idle on the robe-smooth stone,
the horned and beaked heads, emptied by long pain,
watch over the moors;
scooped thin with years,
the upright bodies keep their bench of bone.

Gently we come here, but do not kneel down;
hopelessly human dignity has outgrown
the formal reverence
and makes no pretence
to dominations stranger than our own,

who touch their sides and hands to have of them
solace, by emblem, of the wasting pain
in care found powerless
to protect or bless
children and kindred from the place of stone

in which we, too, obey dictates and crowns,
grown strangers to our own, so simply born
once to a girl
whose big hands held the world
and whose hard peasant knees pressed down the stone.

CORIOLANUS TO VOLUMNIA

Forgive me that I make of love
this terror that can not disprove
its own ambition to be lost
within the passion it has cursed;

forgive me that I make of you
this image of a Fate that knew
what you did not who bore my bones
and lullabied me in the stones;

and, more, forgive what I have done
to own myself your proper son
by fastening this iron mask
on the forgiveness I would ask.

THE BIRTHDAY

Here is the place humanity was made —
fleas in the byre and a rough night outside,
rain swaling down, the puddles in the yard
pitted and flickering, a single star
yellow as ivory crucified on the mist,
the chained beasts crouched like mourners in the straw.

This is the act our centuries have revered —
in occupied territory, ashamed, afraid,
the woman sweating, taut, with rasping breath,
arched on the straw, and urging towards birth
the red, wet, squalling, crumpled Son of Man
that kicked his way into the trap of death.

Angels there may have been, adoring, glad,
but barbed wire waited for the new-born head,
and death by hanging, and contempt, and lies.
The woman lay there after the torn birth,
private with glory on the teeming earth,
God at her breast, a terrible new peace . . .

STATISTIC

Every three seconds some child dies of hunger.
One has just died since this poem began.
Now another is dead. I make my poetry
in a blinding storm of dying man.

Legs sharp as twigs, flesh dinted putty, bellies
huge with gas, mouths scabbed: each way we look
is accusation; man foresaking man
has married nightmare to the hurrying clock

and will not wait to see his kinfolk die.
Their death is not our death. I watch my son
dance for the joy of life. Who shares that joy?
How many children have died since the dance began?

To Claim Her Love

PROTHALAMION AT MIDWINTER
to Sandy and Nora

No longer do we expect
peace on earth,
or more than a transient
modicum of goodwill;
no longer do we suppose
there is anything different
ahead of us or behind us:
conflict is all,

And of our nothingness
nothings must always come,
deaths from starvation or justice,
warfare or shame,
rituals of negation
or false promise,
sacraments of bloodshed
or mutual blame;

Yet there remains to us
one last assertion
of the particular spirit,
of the *nous*,
binding the separations,
blessing order
with a woman and man
in the one house

emulating Eden,
(that luckless garden) ,
but with foreknowledge,
innocence redefined
by mutual pleasure,
mutual compassion,
Serpent and Angel
domestic to the mind

that knows the falsehoods
in all tales of law,
all nursery prohibitions,

and all vows,
yet chooses now
to promise to seek promise
and keep the promise
holy in the house.

It is Midwinter Festival.
The child
leaps from the womb
that he may stretch at Spring;
the Tree of Darkness
burns its gifts of stars;
the earth rewards
the Shepherd and the King.

And it is good
that at this time two friends
should make a wedding,
matching need to need
and love to love
as earth itself asserts
the lurking glory
of the buried seed

and challenges the night
and cold with fire,
with Holly-King,
with Druid Mistletoe,
with myths of Visitants,
and gives a child
new power over
all this world below,

and sky above, and sea,
and every man
and creature, every
fish and beast and bird,
for every wedding
makes a place for birth,
and every birth repeats
that primal word,

which wrought this earth's
explosion into Time,
and split the soul
that here is unified,
the high and low,
the mirror and the face,
the near and far
met in the groom and bride,

who now, in this disconsolate
ruined place,
detritus of original
despair,
make whole what should be whole,
bless what should bless,
and, altering the consistence
of the air,

enable us to breathe,
this day at least,
the clarities and radiance
heart approves
and mind discriminates.
Dear friends, for this
and all, we lay
our blessings on your loves.

THE PRETENCE

The pretence of music to have something to say
in terms of pure structure, the pretence
of the fashionable woman in the way
she walks into the centre of the dance,
are safe from us. No matter how we stick
to calling her smiles cheating, or the lift
of that allegro a disquieting trick,
man's love lives on its myths. Orpheus charmed trees,
and Helen is possible even in times like these.

Perhaps we must accept the pretender's crown,
the salesman's bonhomie, the preacher's grace,
and each woman's carefully made face
or every attitude would be thrown down
and all dependence gone; but if we do,
and you accept my kiss, and I— I, you —
then let our gullibility erect
a complete credo for the intellect
and accept too this fake, this boast, this curse.
True love weds lying and asks no remorse.

NOTHING OF BEAUTY

Nothing of beauty,
(watching the coarse flesh),
rather the relish
of a mutual, gross,
accepting knowledge:
what is true is use —
beauty, that nagging
midnight tooth, no loss.

Unless you gloss it,
(clapping the two bones),
calling the need the beauty,
urging this
to leap philosophies
where many, thrown,
have broken backs
upon the stone that is.

Or if you make it,
(gentling the used flesh),
rather the sharing
of the hungry ghost
no meat may gorge,
that stands aside, calls 'Truth',
'Love', 'Beauty', 'Peace',
and is himself the lost.

CHICK

This rain-wet chick
with her slick vinyl doesn't
in her wink and glisten
sluicing off
the small chill rain
attend to smiles; her eyes
bat gummed-on lashes
blackly at each look

from lecherous middle age
or gaping callow
long-limbed coltishness;
her mouth, a child's
unbruised conception,
wears its careful pink
without intent,
each grey-green iris blank

as eyes in mirrors,
fending off the small,
the raw, the avid
semblances; her steps
make waves in standing pools,
disturb the drowned
brown ghosts of trees and buildings,
click and tap

logistics she,
a theorem without proof,
implies but does not
demonstrate, her chief
accomplishment to feed
our love of doubt
while granting us
occasions for belief.

AN UNCERTAIN MEANING

for Sylvia

Wearing an old coat in the sweat of sun,
uprooting plantains from the not-so-level
length of lawn, the inevitable I
becomes sententious, moral, at the drop
of memory's thinking cap: uprooting all
(perhaps) of canker in the yeasty flesh,
grubbing up each guilt with blackened nails,
or else (another way to twist the key)
humbling the animal under furious light.

That's not what I set out to say. I thought
to send a message out of my sure love,
deliberate as heartbeats, a decorum
of the passionate order your name made,
but this broke in. Outside the sky is grey,
the sun invisible, the lawn still pinned
firmly down with plantains. I've not been
that gardener yet, not grubbed up anything
this ordinary February afternoon.

There may be no connexion, or there may.
Ingenuity suggests the words
came from a hidden prompting, and my love
is less an order than an ordering,
still setting innocence to rights, a beast
covered with all old dreams of hide and hair,
working its heat out, struggling for a place
where penance has brought every kind perfection
and natural impulse lacks its natural flaws.

But such is to disguise the actual thing.
It is not certain what the symbols mean.
Likely enough it looked so cold outside
I had to wear death's coat below the sun
for emphasis of heat, and had to stoop
because the every thought is bedded deep,
and walked the lawn because the flesh is grass
and flesh is asking now. Or maybe not.
At any rate, I send this with my love.

THREE WAYS OF LOVE

I

To claim her love
is to burn all you have
in circlets of bright hair,

watching the knots of smoke
dissolve, drift, break
charmed and enchanter,

till everything's consumed,
lover and loved one
both a mingled ash,

feathers of dissolution
left to the wind's action.

Winds blow where they wish.

II

Ferment of heart
may set the mind apart,
savaging its throes;

a passionate intent
weighing all fortune meant
may get him on his toes,

who, gross and mildly formed,
lunch-dozes, mows the lawn,
has faith and children safe,

or end his quiet life.

III

There is a mirror
in the pool

                    two mirrors

in each other
dazzling

           double sunlight.

ON A SUMMER NIGHT

When in the hot night
cats make
ululation,
soft-pawed
blues lifting
love-hungry
masks to ultimate
ruined moons,

I remember
eyes watching
eyes across
a cafe table,
hands walking
towards each other,
hushed and
delicate as
cats.

SHE, UNREHEARSED

She, unrehearsed in the play, meets
first on the road the cold beggar.
Pity in this her fumbling at her purse
as he cheats frost, blows on cramped cunning fingers.
(Here it begins, god-beggar, woman-purse,
a road of white rime in the Goat's weather.)

She, by the travelled stage, comes
next, and perturbed, on the blind parson
tap-tap at lych-gate, under stone owls
deafened with bells and prayers asks blessing,
(Pity in this the grey maimed shelterers),

under her growing silks a child kicking.
Had she first entered Right, walked
(priest then god) in thc opposite direction,
the Lion summer might have laid her down
barren and armed against love's sovereign action.
(Pity in this, not her but the rehearsed,
treading a known stage, for their lines unspoken.)

THE HEARING

(Englynion Y Clyweit)

Lover, have you learned to hear,
whispered in the secret ear,
Love is all that love should fear?

Have you heard the blackbird sing,
lifting up its burnished wing,
Love is darkness quarrelling?

Have you listened to the sound
of the night owl on its round,
Love is what the vole has found?

Have you heard at end of night
rafters creakingly recite,
Love is burdened by the light?

Have you woken to the spell
rising from the moss-coped well,
Love is Heaven kissing Hell?

Have you turned your head to hear
from the grasses on thc weir,
Love is far, but Death is near?

Has the sudden trodden stone
greeted you with helpless moan,
Love must mourn and lie alone?

Have you heard the plover cry
from the ploughland to the sky,
Love is cloud run careless by?

Have you listened to the snail
chaining leaf with silver trail,
Love is beak and Love is nail?

Have you, tossing in your sheet,
heard the whisper at your feet,
Love is but a garnished meat?

Have you heard within the wave
rearing from the seaman's grave,
Love will drown what Love would save?

Yet, for all this, have you heard
with each dark and warning word,
Love is what God's finger stirred?

ON THE COMMON

Hands twining grasses
mesh the need of words.
The bird above's the lark
that Shakespeare chose.
Now sound is dangerous,
for love's laid its trap;
whatever's said turns yes
to lift her clothes.

Conspiracies of cloud
in wig and shawl
note down the birdsong
and the pandar trees.
She plaits a flower
in the mesh of light,
and light, sub-rosa,
slides above her knees.

In common pastoral
the highway herd
of automobiles
drains unwatched away
towards the spire
on which the weather turns.
The world is Maytime
and she fears I may.

No innocence does more
than her alarm
to grace disorder
with a lovely shame.
The trees around are trees
that Petrarch knew.
The mesh of grasses
wrinkles into flame.

THE WOMAN

Flesh bulges as she drags her corset down,
unloosens brassiere; two swinging tits
nudge the slack belly; hair cascades her frown
and tired eyes; hands smooth the stiffening hips.

Clothes lie disordered on a chair; she bends
to straighten nylons; quagging buttocks shake;
blue veins behind the knees, marks of the brassiere
between the shoulder blades, lift love awake.

Ignorant of beauty, rueful and ashamed
of thick trunk, slack breasts, broad flank, at the glass
she stands on splayed feet, scratching; nervous tremors
ripple the vast abandons of her ass.

Turns to the bed then, reaching for a covering,
her belly wrinkling, unaware of eyes
that bless and reverence her tangled glory
black-bushed between the flaccid marbled thighs,

unaware that this used flesh she squanders,
bullies and hides, this signature of mass,
brings him within the darkness of earth's centre
the vast extremities of crotch and breast

more surely because creased, worn, tensed, and soiled,
it is all creatures' allegory — this
love's own close universe, all humankind
labouring within her hot involving kiss.

CAT AND BIRD

'Kiss me, and if that is old hat
under the moon, be out of date
once in a while, because the tune
is one that has stayed up too late
and falls asleep upon its bars,
childish as kittens, and because
who was it said once every house
is roofed with platitudes like slate?
Kiss me', she said. I heard the cat
moving among the strawberries.

'Tell me, and if you can't think what,
having forgotten, take a shot
at someone's words because the day
here in this room is close and hot
and silence is as full of words
as all your books, and, oh, because
why was it that we bought this house
if not with an erotic thought?
Tell me', she said. I saw the bird
wounding the heavy strawberries.

'Always and always; that, if trite,
could still ring true if we had not
seen each way end, and now, because
we have grown tired of lying late
and early in this watchful house,

playful with memories, and because
we find all music runs to bars,
how long should we keep kisses caught?
Always?' she asked. The cat and bird
wrestled among the strawberries.

Annulets For Eros

WITH PROPER RESPECT

Let us in this pagan Spring
omit no sacrifice
to suasory Priapus,
who, gay and maiden-wise,
lurks in the stagier bars,
and with Edwardian flowers
placates the flesh that lies.

Let us in this casual world
omit no proper rite
to Venus Aphrodite
who decks the busier streets
with eager almost-nudes
prescribing pills or shoes
for the sexually discreet.

In simple and submissive way
let us respect the word
of Eros, poised in winging,
indecorous and absurd,
through our grey firmament
and think to what extent
we might not have occurred.

THE END OF THE NIGHT

A drunk poet in a woman's bed
to keep his fancy warm
at morning kissed her draggled head
and leaned upon one arm

to look at lashes caked with black,
at eyelids greased with blue,
at lipsticked mouth gone smeared and slack,
and all that he could do

was think again, *Warm breasts, warm thighs,*
hot harshnesses of hair,
was think again, *Round rump, tight arms,*
and, staring idly there,

reflect that beauty blurs with use,
until she turned her head
in sleep, and smiled as a child smiles
for comfort of the bed.

HANDFAST

Hand moving where your
hand has moved, I think
your moving hand,
your delicacies of lust,
the turret nipple
lunging to my lip,
the leaping tongue
responding thrust on thrust,

and mingle beard
and beard again to sip
love's ichor in between
cheek-pressing thighs,
and once more watch
the soft mouth softly grip
that rampant rebel
whose one paradise

is raven-haired, brown-skinned,
red-lipped, proud boned,
sighing through orchards
as that Goddess sighs
who in her body knows
each urge of earth
and brings into her bed
all truths, dreams, lies.

ET EGO IN ARCADIA . . .

Laughter we had,
and nakedness, and love,
child-like together till
the sleepless night
waned bright above the lake,
and pride we had
and candour, and that helpless
deep delight
that baffles reason with a
smile or kiss;
pleasure we had, and
pleasure short enough
to live forever
and be loved forever.
Why now should I shrug
that memory off?

THAT AFTERNOON

Wine-drunk and love-drunk both,
we licked and pawed
like puppies, tumbling
warm-skinned on the bed,
teasing impossibilities
with laughter,
mocking intensities,
until you said,

suddenly self-conscious,
O, my love,
we're infants, infants!
and, dry-eyed, I saw
my thick-veined hand,
the crease upon your neck,
and knew love's childhood
hid a bitter law.

HUBRIS

Proud and ashamed
to know my friends all know,
have seen her night-things
in my bedroom, guessed
her perfume in the bathroom,
even, calling
in the morning found her
half undressed,

she still pretends discretion,
leaves the door
unanswered, whispers
on the telephone
as if some insubstantial
passing ghost,
and makes love with such
desperate abandon,

such insistent need,
her climax wrenched
and agonized, her trapped
breath harsh and loud,
that, in possessing her,
I am possessed,
accused, convicted, and
ashamed and proud.

THE SETBACK

Seated, suddenly shamed
upon the bed,
arms crossed on naked breasts,
thighs pressed together,
bowed back frailly ridged,
hair tumbling down,
your anguish at the completeness
of your failure

to enlarge my love
and adoration
into a proper
implement for passion
is misplaced,
for all too often lust's
inhibited by tenderness
in this fashion,

and fearful, pitiful,
denies itself
the brutal strength
required by the occasion.
So dry your eyes, my dear.
Come back to bed.
No conscience can outlast
that warm persuasion.

ACCURSED

Whenever your name
Crops up at work, she whispers,
I can't help it —
suddenly I'm wet!
She stares, huge-eyed,
across thecafé table.
The skin upon her cheeks
is flushed and taut.

And just your name —
not even touching you!
Her lip is trembling.
Tears are in her eyes.
Damn you, she whispers, *Damn you!*
and her hand
upon my hand is hard
and cold as ice.

THE JOURNEY

I missed three trains at least.
Each time I tried
to leave, I turned
and looked at her and stayed,
nostalgic for the damp
warmth of her breasts,
her handled rump, her
woman smell, and, laid

beside her, helpless,
could not say Goodbye,
scared that the sweetness
never would return,
or that, returning
in a different way,
it would not have
the casual ease, the warm

unforced companionship
of this affaire
that in the one night
had unloosed my chains
and freed realities
of love and care,
and travelled farther
than those reaching trains.

ONCE MORE

Once more, once more
come naked to my arms.
Forget that we were players once
and lost
the set, the match. Forget
that later meeting,
you sick, I sour. Forget
the waste, the cost,

and once more, once more
come to my arms,
forgetting everything,
for I forget
all but the essence, all
but love, and love
is everything I never
shall forget.

SATIS EST

Recalling it is enough —
at least for the moment —
her soft moist mouth,
the gentled weight of breasts
with nipples roused, and,
under arms that lift
naked around my neck,
black glistening hairs.

And other hairs, of course,
no longer hidden,
then, at last, the sliding
lips, the clutch
and suck of heat;
recalling it is good,
at least as I read through
her latest letter,

not remembering
her thin high voice,
her taste in poetry,
her perverse opinions,
but her tossed hair
upon the sweat-damp pillow
and my pride,
my splendid stupid pride.

THE PRIMROSE

The primrose watches me
pull down her dress:
stepped from that
gape and wrinkle on the floor,
her hands reach round,
free breasts into their curves,
then scrape down gauze.
Hairs shiver and curl up.

Like me?
                    I like.
                              I smile,
touch tip, touch rim,
then kisssing, hold her,
touching tongue to tongue.
She had not seen a
primrose till that day,
has asked its name
beside the cairn of stones.
Primrose I'd said,
and *Primerole, first Rose,*
sniffing her blossom
with my arrant thorn.

YOUNG

Today you caused, and knew you caused,
the stretching of my secret vein,
the blunt jut of my stiffening heat,
and , innocent of any shame,

you smiled with pleasure, and I felt
your wide eyes strip my body bare,
your unsaid candours show me sheets
for pressures of our tangled hairs.

But I confess, my dear, so young
and bared you were, that shaking thighs
were terrified at all the frank
suggestions of your childlike eyes,

not from extremity of sex,
but that no man alive can prove
the naked absolute you ask
or change the wrecking thrust of love.

CORRESPONDENCE

I touch your nipples with my tongue,
first one and then the other, and
they stiffen . . . Do they stiffen, dear,
as in your far-off alien land
you read these words? Do they recall
(as I recall) those stolen nights
and secret mornings? Or do they,
secured from amorous delights
within their taut imprisoning cups,
grown blandly placid, rest unstirred
and imperturbable although
I touch them in each loving word
and softly suck and gently squeeze?
Are they impervious to this?
Or, as you read, do they reach up
their swollen buds to meet my kiss?

Bestiary

THE BIRDS

Out of my childhood birds
pick at the laid stones
cemented together: lime,
(lime for thc dead ones' bones),
sand, (sand for the time
that drags and drains away),
and water (oh water, water)
bonded them where they lay,
fastened them, froze them, fixed them,
yet out of my childhood these
birds pick at the laid stones,
roost in the nailed trees.

EAGLE

Vertigo is my territory, Man
only another movement, another shift
in the arrangement of shadows beneath my shadow,
angular, thick-boned, cumbersome, and bad meat.

I do not trouble him or the larger kind,
having no love of eating on the ground;
I kill what I can bring into my height,
what I can raise up until, terror-stunned,

they watch the dwindling of their day, perceive
the small earth small, self-cancelling, and share
the shock that is the last discovery; here
they learn abandonment of every word

and are self-rent before I rend and eat
what they already have forgotten, locked
on fear and splendour. Image me as God.
I am the final judgement and the rock.

MOOR HENS

Once I knew a pond
where water hens
fluttered and sputtered;
it was over the wall
from the old schoolhouse,
dark in Blashill's field;
Blashill is dead now
and the pond filled in.

Somewhere, however,
in the heart of my sleep,
wings flutter and slap those waters
and thorns crouch down
above my reflected face
and someone calls me
in from the field
afraid that I may drown

as I can't drown now,
being old and large
for the shallows of such a place
yet I know the urge
to hear "Come away, come away —
the water is deep!"
for the wings in the shallows beat
and the face stares up.

WART HOG
for Jack Coughlin

Moon-tusked, wrenching at roots,
I dream of women.

Once there were sacred boars
in the sacred wood,

eaters of corpses,
guardians of the groves

under the wand of the goddess.
Now I grub,

trample, and squeal,
bulk-shouldered, warted, haired

rank as the sweat of terror,
sour as shame,

guardian of no ritual
but the thrust

through darkness
of the bald horn of the rnoon.

WARNING WITH EMBLEMS
for Marianne Moore, a more delicate fabulist

I

The earth is
dark. I see
owls in your
palm

and they are
birds of
love that
eat raw meat

and wait upon
the moon;
       a
grave dark man

stands in your
thumb and
strokes it till you
cry

II

Happiness hurts like
love; joy
thrusts through the knot of nerve
a nail

shiny as terror;
delight splits
the heart in the side
and breath ends

pinned and jumping,
a small death
compared with some,
but, resurrected,

the scars remain,
and delight chills
near in each
smile we turn from,
frightened.

III

Natural morality
exudes
rank odours.
The cicada sings

as it sucks juices;
bitten, mauled,
envied, robbed, it
drinks, sings

joy of the short life,
makes before
summer is done
dried meat for winter.

IV

This insolent hand
belongs to
murderer Love.

You had not known?
Know now.
Your death is
coming.

Hard fingers
touch, then,
gently terrible,
close.

Not that!
Not now!

Yes, now.
Yes, now.
Yes,
       this

V

Here is the fall of the
body toppling
down in a straight dive,
hands held

stiff as a prayer
face cowled
in the slippery muscles,
the wet shoulders,

lips firm,
eyes nerved
ready for blindness
at the shock,

the sudden throat
of the flower, down
which silence alters
and time grows.

VI

The cicada cannot
be roused to anger,
cannot even
suspect enemies,

and when it sings
it cannot hear
anything else;
when caged it flies

upwards, beats
itself to death,
is lured by applause,
short-lived,
dies quickly.

GOAT

I have a name for it.
I smell rank
to nostrils of morality.
I thrust home,
however shrill the bleat.
My eye is red,
my hairy tangle
knotted stiff with balm.

I know my end.
Exuberant with seed,
I mount thc universal
pulse, whose heat
offends your niceties,
and makes you fear
the blinding energies

of lunge and rut,
and use me as an emblem
of the rogue,
the fool, the outlaw,
and, extolled by flame
on midnight moorlands,
the forbidden god
of naked sorceries,
those ancient dreams

I do not have to dream.
No tether can
efface the name I sign
on field and yard;
circling the centre,
I possess my need,
and, ribald, eat
the rubbish of thc world

to feed the fury
that the world proclaims,
derides, disguises, cheats:
I am that thing
shame hides and halters
till it bursts its bonds,
and in your farmyards
dance upon my string.

LIZARD

This is our land.
The soil contracts and cracks.
The rivers break like twigs.
The dust absorbs
the cries of birds.
A horse's giant skull
stares from a rock,
the gaps in reason bared.

This is our time.
The bullet in the brain

implodes reversions
as the dying mind,
encountering desert,
stretches out its hands
through mirage
where the cities of the plain

have folded into sand,
and we lift up
blunt saurian heads,
our ancient patience paid
at last, at last rewarded.
Power has burned
the final sun
into the final grave

and death itself has changed.
We grow. We rise.
We lurch through continents
after monstrous flies.

SLUG

I am a mouth,
a wet mouth, moving

slow suctions
of stiff leaves

into my miriad teeth,
eating

green till the bared veins
stand out,

quiver, brittle,
and, tensed, snap.

I am both he and she,
one slippery

muscle, the pulse
of absolute darkness,

mouthing my eggs
upon decay,

and, humped, sliming
wet silver

at every surge.
I ripple, glisten

black, stroking
the prone surface

into my hunger,
each caress

heart's need and ruin,
every thrust

a slow comment
on love and love.

SCORPION

Black-laced, black-beaded, delicate, this creature
sidles the floors of our furtive amorous leisure.

holding her claw like a bible, a black-beaked book,
to counter the jut at the groin, the breathless shock

and the pulsing responsive moan. We who go bare
into our pleasures have earned her clothed reminder

and the sudden starting sweat on the pallid face,
hands leaping, frightened, to startled mouth and breast,

as she scuttles away, is vanished. For this little mother,
our black-gloved, bombazined, mute, intrepid warrior,

a crack in a stone is enough, or a split in a beam.
She sees us clear and sees us small. Our screams,

grimacing rictus, arching our backbones, forced
out in this haven of practised, compassionate lust

are nothing to her but echoes; and yet to stamp
her flat is to stamp flat what gives our limp

impulse its feral cunning, its local ardour.
There is no less necessity of order

than of indulgence; always she plays a part,
lurking, bright-eyed, black-capped, to arrest the heart.

LOBSTER

I wear bone.
I am bone-worn,
shifter of sands,
weed-green,
stone-mottled,
saw-clawed.
I break bone open
to break bone.

Lodged
in a storm-firm house,
hidden,
salt with despairing,
my probed will
pierces the curtains
of thick water,
choking with sand
and crushed shell

here on the edge
of a black world
where continents shelve
to a long fall;
I lift my bone, my claw,

my fierce
armoured suffering

under the pull
of dark planets
your sleep-naked
hungers tug
through a black wave.
I am the claw
in the wet crotch,
the rock-dweller
that eats love,

the ultimate need.
My eyes steer,
depraved by moons,
through veils of water.
At each death
I am mantled blood
washing the heart
that dreams of armour.

THE CAT
for Sam

The cat stood under the lilac.
It was black.
The sky was blue, the grass green, and it stood
black under the lilac
that was lilac
under the sky that was all over blue.

No matter that the way we say is how
the thing is in the mind, a proof of sorts
that where we stand and look is what we are,
sometimes a black cat stands black under lilac
and the grass is green, the sky unknown.

BEAR

Tall girl, tall boots,
short skirts, black leather . . .
                          Slap !
The thin line cuts air cleanly.
Damp hands clap.
White faces shine.
The animal, erect,
wet-eyed, blunt-muzzled, drools.
Sweat mats the packed
harsh hairs, as,
                  blonde,
she swivels on her heel,
disdain charged with excitement,
and appeals
for silence, tension.
                      Will she bring it off?
The giant leans into the imminence, stiff.
She lifts the whip.
Trained muscles tense.
                      It comes,
the climax and the drumroll.
                          Finished, numb,

discarded by her smile
and spotlit charms,
he slumps into release.
                      She lifts her arms,
triumphant, glistening.
Her breasts are taut.

The crowd roars animal into the night.

SPIDER

A *Saint*, they said, A *Saint*!
And there she lay,
naked, entranced in her cell.
I wove my web
between the stiff rapt thighs.
They held their breaths

in awe to see
the cunning of the veil

I spun from the hate in my gut
on that spotless place,
for I am the Lady of Traps —
my every lover's
post-coital sadness
meets my bite;
I hoe their legs at the joints;
I crush up armour.

Yet she lay easy,
breathing but unmoving,
trapped by her soul into stillness.
I ate flies
between the lips of her vulva.
She never stirred
but the once to whisper *Beloved* . . .
Was I the adored?

I, the Lady of Silence?
I choke mouths,
blind eyeballs, shroud the tombs.
I am the dream
that drifts through palpitations.
I slide my net
across the coupling buttocks
of Mars and Venus,

the agent of shame and wisdom.
I crouch at the centre
garnering paralysis, waiting . . .
Could I be dear
to any trapped or victim?
Who is the victim?
The buzzing of prayers has ended.
I scuttle to supper.

TOAD

Seated on well-lip,
toad and lady,
blotched skin, thin tongue
flicking at flies,
white skin, round flank,
eyes of compassion
and dry-mouthed hunger
thought to kiss.

Who, save in the
nightmare of country
wisdom, would earn
the wart on the lip
for hope of the jewel!
As she bent down
the moon was hidden,
the trees stood still.

Here was her fortune.
Her heart shook.
Her small breasts trembled
within her gown.
Her breath was musky.
She bit her lip.
Unblinking, the toad
watched her stoop down

then leapt into darkness.
He was darkness.
'Lover', she cried, 'Ah Lover'
as she fell,
the moonlit well-head above her
bright as a jewel,
the leap of her tongue
an echo down the well

of every darkness
gathered in every need.
They found her at morning,
head split by a stone.

There is no prince in this country,
only mirrors
kissing within the darkness
where we drown.

BED BUG

They kiss, fumble.
I wait in wood,
attendant. Sheets
roar, slide,
clatter. Sweat
streams at their grunts.
A hand crashes
above my head

and buttocks heave.
I smell perfumed
hair, perfumed
hot skin
and growing stifles
of wet musk,
slimes of the first world's
first seeping

wrought by the gross
seismic wrench
of time's convulsion;
I crouch, wait.
Heels thud.
Hands batter.
There is a cry
repeated, trapped

in a conviction
older than
rag, wood, or stone.
I bide my time.
Stillness . . . stillness . . .
I scuttle, crawl,
fasten upon
one slumbering limb,

and slow, slow,
glut, swell,
reddening, heaving
the deeper sleep
of earth's hunger.
They sigh, dream.
I feed on ignorance
like hope.

HOMO SAPIENS

At last the animals
come out into the sun,
carrying with them the darkness
but no moon,

gradual, wise, and appetent,
their eyes
patient and watchful.
From bird-crowded skies

trills, whistles, shrieks attend us.
From the sea
Leviathan lifts his huge head,
and we,

dying in deserts, die
an unforgiven
desolate, cramped, drab death,
unblesscd, unshriven,

knowing that all we proved
is what's unknown
unthought, unfelt, unseen;
we are our own

complete negation, dark.
We are what's left
for the hill fox's bark,
the lion's cough.

In Ireland

FOR DUBLIN WITH LOVE

To fall in love with Ireland
is to court
a ghost with the smile of a mother,
the eyes of a girl
giddy with singing,
and the white skin of a clerk
intent with brush
on the cracking page of a Missal.

I have been betrayed
into this liaison
by the formidable Uncles,
cavern-toned,
stamping the boards of their stage,
announcing heroes,
pouring me through the city
on bell-tongued tides.

Hunted, I cannot escape her,
no more than Joyce
recalling the curve of her buttock
in Zurich streets
and mouthing his lover's babble,
inventing words
to trouble the wry-necked clerics
above their books.

No one can ever escape her
once her head
has turned in the turning sunlight,
gold and grey
as changing silks of the curtain
dropped across
the sun from a cloud of mourning
above the sea.

No one resembles her. No one.
Byzantium's been
outclassed by her streetgirl dance,
and Ilium veiled
in the dignity of her suffering,

Rome reduced
to dust by her narrow insistence,
her generous smile.

I have been trapped,
and I tangle traditional robes
in postures of adoration,
skin my fingers
on strings that snap like a mousetrap
or hang slack
on a harp that abuses my eardrums
and cricks my neck.

Nothing as funny has happened
to please her for years,
not since George Moore learned the Gaelic
and tried to skip
to the sound of an unstrung fidil
in County Mayo;
or that beanpole Anglo-Irishman
launched his ship

on a tide of prosaic pretensions,
a hooker of Galway
rhyming the prices of fish;
or Yeats, in a fury
of scholarly misdirection,
made Blake an O'Neill,
and sat Urizen down in Kiltartan
to spell a Rann.

But laughter has never perturbed her.
Hot-eyed fools,
innocent in their passion
and transformed
by urgent ridiculous loyalties,
have her forgiveness;
even the maddened sobrieties
of the learned

can be excused, then forgotten,
while steel-eyed censors
raging with purity,

burning the *News of the World,*
and watchful for mention of underwear,
are admitted
equally into the company
of Saints and Scholars.

Indiscriminate Ireland,
Ireland crazed
by the hearts affections,
the pure zest of the mind,
the long dance of the tongue,
the remembered suffering,
Ireland innocent, vivid,
wondering, bland,

troubles me like the drink.
The formidable Uncles
brought me into her house,
and in sonorous tones
said something inappropriate;
on the wall
was a photograph of Maud Gonne
with a boss-eyed hound,

and a purple Paul Henry landscape.
I looked. I listened.
A voice rose out of an inkwell
and talked of graves.
A bottle of Inisfree Water
whispered *Thalatta,*
and someone in snot-green silk
took a flag and waved

to the tenor elongating syllables
till they festooned the
room with a seaweed of ribbons
upon which bells
tolled Angelus,
and seven Sisters of Mercy
told seven tales of Saint Patrick
to seven gulls

come in from Lord Nelson's shoulder.
I looked. I listened.
A man in an ulster
ate oranges from a plate
entirely covered in shamrock,
spitting the golden
pips in a rage of humility
at his fate.

And a black-bearded printer
piled sugarlumps into a dolmen
from which sweetness dropped,
drip by drip, on the upturned mouths
of sixteen poets, seven playwrights,
and forty-five scholars
engaged in outlining the final,
the ultimate truth

about Synge, about Yeats, about Swift,
about Tara, commenting
in between drips
on the terrible state of the nation.
I looked and I listened.
And then one remarkable Uncle
led me outback to the stars
that filled the spaces

between the grey decorous squares,
and I heard a singing.
The words were no matter;
they came clear and keen
as a flute across lake water,
as if the mountains
around the city
hunched to a secret tune

that no one could hear but the once.
I heard it, listened
to something still and chill
from the riot heart;
a blackbird under a hedgerow

might have known it,
or a curlew high on the moorland;
wilder than art,
and stranger than music,
it wandered like a woman
wandering, remote with love,
an unending garden,
impersonal in her possessing.
It soared, it fluttered,
delicate, vibrant, absurd
as the heart is absurd

always when touched or abandoned.
It was that moment
Ireland turned her head
and I caught the gleam,
stood there, ridiculous,
clumsy with alien language,
dropping my half eaten syllables
on the stones,

and wiping my mouth with a sleeve
that tasted of Guinness,
and feeling the wind round my heart.
Remote, absurd,
that sweetness lingered and lingers.
Back from exile,
I have made this poem
that the ghost may return.

SWANS SLEEPING
for Elizabeth Havelock

All the swans are asleep, and I remember
Gogarty giving the Liffey a pair of swans,
remember the children of Lir, remember
Leda under those white beating wings,

as a man remembers what there is
of childhood left in stray corners of the house

his age has made habitual. It is,
perhaps, a condition of the evening's peace,

here by the sauntering couples, that no thought
or myth or dream should risk a turning back
to those absurd heroics, yet I had thought
so many here had known the city's wrack,

Pearse's set face, all those broken necks,
the looting rabblement, the spraying guns,
no swans could ever sleep, but would curve necks
continually through greens and browns and duns

of moving water, feeding on the flow
as Jove stooped into Leda, to provide
love, war, and prophecy, a continual flow
of high homeric gestures to deride

the easy smiling couples that stroll past
the root-gripped river bank with idle stares,
as we, too, stroll, engrossed in a dead past
between the violent shadows of the trees.

SONG AT TWILIGHT

Backside strapped
and ear sermoned,
I heard blackbirds
in half light
on my way prepwards;
great chestnuts
cluttered with candles
shook leaves.

Schoolboy faces
and holy fathers
recall that bitter
keen delight
in Dublin suburbs;
subdued files

trooping past railings
send waves

roaring through thirty
years of hearing
different blackbirds,
darker texts,
to flood chestnuts,
light candles,
echo the lonely
blessing asked.

WOODTOWN MANOR, DUBLIN
for Garech de Brun

The peacock cries.
I tug nettles
free of the black earth,
haul thc rose
clear of encumbrance.
The stone house
shimmers in sunlight.
The road swerves

through muddled meadows
to far mist
dwindling the city.
I retreat,
straighten my back,
my hands cut,
stung, bitten,
my shirt wet

black with the sweat
of more years
than years can number.
The peacock cries
again, again;
the rank grass
drags at the thousand
trailing eyes

as earth has always
dragged. Heat
drums in my skull.
I gasp, glut
on the cold wine.
The bird's cry,
full-throated,
tears the heart,

rips at the stones,
the cry of pride
alone with history.
I bend
again to the tangle
of the green,
wrenching with ancient
useless hands.

FIRST ENCOUNTER
in Homage to Robert Flaherty

The first film that I saw
    was *Man of Aran.*
Nine years old, I sat in the
    dark and stared
at the relentless seas,
    the raking stones,
the coracles. They'd thought it
    was *Treasure Island*

and were disappointed for me.
    The Atlantic
broke through the watching rows
    of the holy room,
drowning, battering.
    The next week
it was Long John Silver,
    pieces-of-eight, and Pew

ancient and blind as Raftery!
    But I carried

Aran there in my head,
        and palm-fronds shook
to the gasp of breakers;
        hunched up in the dark
of everywhere, my tensed hands
        gripped at rock,

exultant, secret.
        Though the holiday sands
were printed upon the screen
        with swords and spades
and parrotting adventurers,
     behind
their dwarf games walked the
        giant of the wind

I knew ahead of me.
        The murdering treasure
shone like candy.
        Swords and ships and guns
faded against the rock.
        I was a rock.
Blindly I walked out,
        Aran, to the sun.

CLARE ABBEY

'Remember me when I am dead
and simplify me when I'm dead.'
        — Keith Douglas

Item, skull. A clutter of dry bones.
Several snapped and broken. At least one gnawed.
The Abbey window has no glass: the nave
is grass; the tombs are black holes fringed with nettles.
Wire prevents the sheep, at least; the tourists
hold their cameras clumsily at bad angles.

Simplify me. This is much too tangled
up with roots and gullshit.
Gulls come in
across the cliffs when winds blow up, and spit

white on the sepulchres, arraign the tower
in harsh voices.
Still, there are no snakes
since Patrick sent them packing,
and no rats.

What I was is nothing to you now
and could make memory difficult. I'd say
an easy lie is best.
Call me a poet.
That's an approximation few will care
enough about to doubt
or look me up
along the dark stacked corridors.
Explain
my life as dates
(Born Then, Died Then tells all)
and close this damned great gap:
I look so small
and complicated fools might think to search
for evidence of love affairs, or pride,
or sudden dangerous solitudes, and learn
more of me than I know.
I do not know
what happened or what mattered.
Keep me dead
and unacknowledged; I ask nothing more.
Simplify me. Then at last my name
will be the thing I was,
a moment's noise
you have no need to dignify or share.

SUIBHNE REDIVIVUS

Constructing my poem
like a pint of porter,
a drop too lively, a drop sour
to freshen, then flatten
and make all creamy,
more of a curate than a seer
in this snug study,

the brass banded
pumps of metaphor well worn
by the clutching fingers,
the calendar
numbered to death by the black phone,
here I am, working,
smoke and chatter
blinding as always, the hard stuff
heady as ever,
the Powers golden,
the Harp just lucid and wild enough,
when who comes in
but the ghost of Suibhne
rattling the keys to his new Ford,
freshly befeathered.
"To hell with trees.
It's maybe a great yoke for a bird,
but never a man",
he says, "I'm trying
Dublin City, the new attraction!
A little mott
in O'Connell Street
said there was plenty of conversation
the way I'd want it.
Being a poet
myself, I'm in chase of a few writers
quick with the rhyme
for a good drink,
but everywhere they are saying '*Jazus,
we've none of that.
It's all the pictures
and Telefis Eireann now for them,
and off to America
every minute
reciting to those Hollywood women.
The old ones are dead.
You remember Mangan?
There was a man with a fine thought!
And Yeats now, Yeats
was a class of man
you wouldn't be wrong to call a poet.
But your man now
is a different creature.*'

That what they're saying". He flaps one wing
over his eyes
and has another.
The old fellow is near to crying.
What can I tell him?
The sad madness
for everything bygone's in his eye.
Names won't touch him.
Young men
are only schoolboys. The old are dry,
and desiccated
or else he'd know them
off by heart. "Then again", he moans,
"the little mott said
the Dail was filled
with fine talkers, but just the once
when I got there
not a man was stirring,
and a fellow I met in Kildare Street
said *'That's all finished.*
Since Mick Collins
met his end there's been none of that.
And Dev's an old one now.
There's nothing
left of the real stuff anymore.
All they're after
is drawing their money
and maybe making a small law
once in a season
and writing letters
about the economy of the nation.
Parnell, now,
there was a thinking one,
but the priests put him well out of action'
That's what I'm told!"
And he picks a feather
out of his elbow to draw trees
in the spill on the bar.
What can I answer?
A great sadness is in his eyes,
and his lip trembles.
I could say "Triumph
resolves its clamour and learns Art".

or maybe get him
to read Kinsella,
Kavanagh, Clarke, or perhaps start
him off on Flann O'Brien,
Beckett,
the painters, the actors; but why spoil
a good bitterness,
stop a hunger
feeding its passion to the soul?
Why not listen?
I smile. I listen.
"I was a king", he says, "the wance,
and a Ruler of Kings . . . "
His eye, unfocussed,
burns with the liquor of Romance . . .
"And a poet", he says,
"when poets were fellers
you'd take off your hat to down the street.
And still a poet:
Wait while I tell you
the latest little bit I wrote
on Stephen's Green
as a crow came over . . .
He clears the phlegm, takes a good sight
on the top corner
beyond the vodka,
rustles his thinking, and comes out
with four Hear-All-Ye's
and seven sighings
of soft rain over the long green hills,
and a number of random
saints and blackbirds
hearing the Monastery bells
as Kathleen passes,
an Old Woman
seeking her bit of turf to put
the warmth under
a broth, while playing
a sad harp for the men shot,
and smiles, waiting.
I say nothing.
He lifts up both his trembling wings
and knocks a table over,

roaring
the holiness of the heart's affections,
the sweet simplicities
of the gael,
the tender-heartedness. Why laugh?
Slowly he drinks
the placating porter.
Mystically, he lurches off
and I watch him flapping
albatross-like
down the roadway, gathering speed
as cars skid wildly
into the windows
(the garda dance like they're going mad),
and then with a heave
bounce, lurch, and sudden
thrust he is up and away, gone
over the roofs —
I'd say heading
West and likely to make Boston
well by morning.
And now, turning
back to what's left of the night's composure
I pull some lively
and some sour,
compose the poem, construct the future.

AN IRISH ALBUM

1. RENAISSANCE

Mother of myths, the old wonder,
soft syllabling it in the back room
of a tumbling history; quaint tales
tacked on the coat of Colleen Bawn

draggled through ditches; real speech
brought back alive, alive alive-o,
to strut in Dublin; Ireland free
and it still afther playin' the slave

with a squinty syntax, the bould cratur,
takin' a drop at the soft hands
of the fine lady, and Misther Yeats
bewildered entirely; a grand man

and he talking . . . Book of the People,
people meaning the kicked clown
painting up bruises, the fool nigger
giving himself a fool name,

habit of centuries . . . Curtain UP !
The blackface minstrels, the green fools,
authentic music from bogged harps,
Renaissance standing with proud smile

at the simple sweetness, the wise words
of Kiltartan Workhouse, the damp walls
bloody with spittle, Kathleen, blackface,
coughing her guts through Tara's Halls.

2.   THE APPLE

Drogheda grey in a grey wind,
the streets empty, I play pilgrim
across to the church to find fruit
of the long rotten tree of Tyburn.

Small on the altar, a yellow apple
wrinkled and shiny, Blessed Plunkett's
head rests, a bland reminder
of kicking crowds, another martyr

good for the books, but old, cold,
the golden head, like the gold bird,
remote in artifice. Who'll pretend
grief for a Phoenix burned out,

a symbol withered? The grey winds
course through Drogheda's grey dust,
breathless with futures. The head sits
emptied and still. The winds pass

Spenser's century, Cromwell's, Pitt's,
but Holy Ireland, History galloping
by her, stumbled, paused, picked
up the apple, is still running.

3.   DITCH LOGIC

Under a Kerry hedge, light shaking
holy emblems of dogrose, briar,
and raindrop silver, the gaunt Father
spelled out Suffering, every letter

another footfall to stop the breath
at God's Wisdom who kept such holy
servitude for the pure Irish,
surely a chosen and flailed people

blessed by revilings and persecutions,
children to sweetly cry Hail Mary
under the blackbird, humble knees
on burned earth at the curlew's cry

through mist drifting. I walk Ireland
listening, suffering the same mists
threaded by music, the same words
but from a plump and different priest

with a house of statues, a cord of candles,
a bloody heart on the great door:
The poor are always with us, blessed:
God is opposed to Medicare.

4.   THE RETURN OF CASEMENT

Casement returns. Already stories
of miraculous preservation
trouble the papers; lime could not
rot, nor clay sour his sweet bones.

This I believe, for a man should
accept whatever surpasses fact
with purest vision. Why doubt?
Practice in faith becomes perfect

blinding clarity, all Truth
a lake of mirrors improving light
with dear refraction. As for Casement:
whether or not thc worm and rot

gouged or the lime burned, doesn't matter.
Reverence transforms its every use,
and better this tyrant-hating gentle
knight than the usual crouched recluse.

5.   GEASA

Forbidden drink, the arms of women
about his neck, and lewd words,
Murphy, no less than Conaire trapped
by rule of the long-plumed King of Birds,

awaits fury, a great thirst
black in his throat, a dry mouth
aching for softness, a small sad
blasphemy whistling in his breath

as darkness nears and the wild horde
of hound-voiced geese on northward wings
announces destiny, priests gathering
watchful as crows for the last things.

6.   FALLGUY OF THE WESTERN WORLD

I take up my pen . . . (pauses, scratches,
fumbles a bottle from a cupboard . . .)
Ancient Ireland . . . (eyes glazing,
gives more Powers to his elbow) . . .

Scholars and Saints . . . (abandons, crumples,
hats head, macs back, is off out
to the Pearl Bar, car radio
jiving sweetly among grey streets

young ankles skip and bottoms bobble . . .
corks on a dangerous tide rising;
three Hail Marys against that
and all lechery ! Later, easing

primal flux up a black alley,
steaming the wall, in a thin voice) . . .
Take me home . . . Kathleen . . . poor bloody
(sobbing) *get of the sad Irish . . .*

WHO WEEPS FOR DEDALUS?

I

Silence, Exile, Cunning. A sham boast,
his long tongue clicking like a two-hinged door
to let her grey streets in, his fingers full
upon her: and what cunning can adore
so openly, so inwardly! The bite
of inwit was their wedding flea each night.

Nor he alone but others, ruined, spoiled,
beggared, crazed, poxed. What a wench is this
can be supremely nymph, colleen, or mott,
nun, vestal, courtesan, aunt, mother, miss,
or mistress; any shift is one she'll take
to twist the silence through a new heartbreak.

Four husbands she has had among the rest,
some say at one time, and some one by one.
Monastery and Castle roofed in two;
a third put up his money at an Inn
as gunfire knocked the streets, while number four
leaned, and leans yet, against the cunning bar,

disreputably still, mind on a horse,
eyes bright with accidie. It's here she'll stay
the world out now. All other beds are cold;
her mouth is thirsty, and her eyes, as grey
as any fabled queen's or murdered stone,
mock history for the centuries it has done.

II

She weeps For Dedalus. She lifts
head high in weeds by greenest of canals,

her handmaids. Drowned as anyone is drowned,
they say he sleeps upon his fathered bed
fathoms under foam, and all the saints
may from their Paulpits practice on the brass.

Who would not weep for Dedalus? She mourns
innumerably, and even if no words
loom darkly in the dead glass of his hand,
she yet, the kissed and cuddler of the dead
from Oisin on, enfolds him; still he lives
and nectar pure with oozy licks he laves

while curates pull the engine. Unfrocked priest,
descutcheoned duke, and bankrupt banker, host
to all the past he isn't, here his head
is meddled on the ribbon that she's led
all this bull in by, careless if she loose
more myths to mouth, call chaos into place

as long as ebbflows, tidesturn, while timends
with towels on and no more births resound.

III

Allwise the elegiac night it is;
each eve's All Hollows to the goats that work
this urnshent city of so moony dead;
hear in the gordian straits a fidil plies
its harmonies while on Saint Starving's Groin
the midnote corpses wrestle: illstars know
allwise thc elegiac night it is.

Eelwoes the ruining river runes and keens;
the mummeries gripe togather weir the stops
acurse the groaned canaille to Bigot's Treat
wring out like hawsers heaves; he leans, she liens
lo on the purrypat, recurling all
posed wards and locks; though hewman dies may end
eelwoes the ruining river runes and keens.

Wholewars and holeways we drown under words,
the beg or smile, the dune or the undawn;
though impures foul and notions louse their why

and ovary servilization brakes lake bards
whose patterns mute the gael, and, though betried
by her again, agone in mournlit years
wholewars and holeways we drown under words.

SHEM ACCOMPANIED

Hawking and spitting at the bar of the dead,
it's Shem the penman has time in his throat;
though not enough to gob the sawdust dark
it sours in all he's drinking, and the dead
are listeners to the long lap of his throat
that might sing birds out of the burning park

but his tongue's iron cold, a clicked-home sneck.
Not one squeak peeps, and he'll let nothing out,
especially to the dead. Time jerks a cough
but can't shape syllables or stretch his neck
into truth's cock-crow. Blood sweet in his stout,
here's Shem the penman fighting glory off

by keeping secret, for no other word
or gesture can rejoinder thus, or stand
in grinning triumph over ratstooth so,
or state more lucidly: Take no man's word
and give none yours. Fame is the dirtiest, and
no less, at last, tongue-tied and out-at-elbow.

THE RETURN OF SUIBHNE

It was on a summer's evening.
I was listening
to my own head making music
from chinking glass
and regretting I couldn't whistle
when Mad Suibhne
stalked into the bar,
in feathers from head to ass,

chirruping like a sailor.
I recognized him
immediately
from the rattle of his lung
and the one eye round as a marble.
He called the curate
something monstrous
and roared for another one

to which he applied the eye,
and its golden whirlpool
whistled back as he stared.
He husked: "I see
the fierce potato
pushing its milk-white fingers
into the womb of the world,
destroying pity.

This is the mandrake monster !
When it screamed,
tugged from the blackened earth
by a wicked hound,
seven centuries died
and a people vanished
into the stetch of corruption,
holding hands

hopelessly up to the light;
this was the emblem
snug in the pocket of lust
when Circe winked
the voyagers into swine,
the deadly message
stitching up the lips
of rhetorical flesh.

"This", he rasped, "is the god !"
And from the pocket
of his heron-ribbed flank
he pulled a withered
spud with the face of a woman.
"Shan Van Vocht",

he muttered, "and tinker Houlihan's
wrinkled daughter,

Ireland, Ireland, Ireland!"
I crossed my fingers,
my legs, and myself very quickly
and, spilling slightly,
leaned through a hover of hiccups
to answer back
in tones of unreasonable reason,
but he had sidled

off through the gap in logic
and was seated
hunched as a crow
at the far end of the bar,
pouring a little hot water.
I followed, lurching
on account of uncrossing my legs,
but had not got far

when weakness overtook me
with sudden abandon
of speech and the use of my knees.
He gave a chirp
of gloomy satisfaction,
folded his wings
about his enormous belly
and fell asleep

like a child on the breast of its mother.
I mouthed for words
but nothing came out but a whistle.
I'd meant to claim
Tradition, History, Scholarship,
Beauty, Religion,
but slowly his figure,
the colour of storm-swept stone,

began to alter and blur
till all remaining
was a shimmer of mist,
an empty glass,

and a leather-brown wrinkled potato.
I have the potato
here on the end of my watch-chain,
just in case . . .

A RATHMINES EVENING
to Ann Cluysenaar

Rathmines clocktower as near
as a great watch lugged from a fob,
big as a child's moon; you unlock the door
and centuries creak back upon the hinge:
a room Swift might have known, a monkish bench,
ten-spindled chairs, a wide bare wooden floor.

Solitude has made this room
and the walled garden where we walk;
snails carting houses across stone
that dark makes harder for the unsure tread
remind us both of something we'd forget;
my arm about you is a deadening bone.

On the marbled mantlepiece
a bronze girl that your father cast
looks out at dark; the loose-framed windows
rattle reflections back at where we stand
between the centuries; your hand is cold,
and cold as comfort the green river flows

time under bridges two miles
north of our nudging Rathmines clock
with drifting histories, who cannot feel
more than the desolation which we share
in being dwellers of a city where
the future flickers and the past is real,

and she is kneeling as if bronze
were what God made her for, upheld
naked, inscrutable, and weary, hands
clasped at the nape, ten pigs of childlike toes
too tamed to wriggle; desolation aches
within her pride. Who gives what she demands?

AT EMMET'S GRAVE

for Liam Miller

What could be less heroic? Rusted nails
about a slab of rainswept wrinkled stone,
bleached white enough, but letterless, unless
the pocks and seams are script, their language gone,
forgotten utterly. I watch the stone.
Who was it said a beauty had been born?

That was a different country, different men,
though just as dead now, and for similar dreams.
Hung askew at one end of the rails
an iron label says half what it means,
the rest absolved by rust. Undecked by fame,
here are Robert Emmet, Wind and Rain —

Three Elementals I might say, but that
such might come near to challenging the ban.
Let No Man Write My Epitaph. These words,
if words they are, were written by no man,
but scribbled out by time and chance alone,
as if the stone itself would mark the stone

with something to be stared at, questioned, guessed.
Before the trees made letters maybe this
was how the sandribs or the troubled pool
extruded syllables. He could not miss
remembrance any more than in this place
wind can avoid the stone or sodden grass,

but staked no claim as hero. That at least
he could avoid. The hollow brazen head
he plotted under maybe taught him that.
The last offence we practice on the dead
is how we summarise, for histories need
what wind and rain supply here, Emmet dead.

A SAINT OF THE LAND

Names are no matter. Bony-kneed,
he stabbed earth many times a day
above this desolate lake or that,
contemptuous whether lice or dirt
or fever carried him away
so long as one of them took heed.

A composite portrait of the head
would show eyes more of hawk than dove.
a jawline sharp-edged as a rock,
and red lips full enough to look
eager for more erotic love
than that of his hard hermit bed.

And stories would be of the sins
he put aside, and of the way
the High King listened in his Hall,
of cripples healed, blind seeing, all
the trees and wells and stones he lay
his hand upon. Death's rictus grins

now at the tale, as we may grin
who, buying postcards at the cell,
or well, or chapel, have not felt
the muscles of our heartbeat melt
in terror of a swinging bell
that gathers all our moments in

as he was gathered who, here, there,
called this or that, became the tale
the Guidebook prints. He lived, then died,
for Truth, and even if he lied
or was mistaken, did not fail
to leave that courage on the air.

The Climbing Wave

TODAY

The whole of this
long day I dwelt
upon a lady
lithe with love

and by the brightness
of her eyes
discovered evidence
to prove

the frightening
hypothesis
that there is no way
to escape

the desperation
of my need
or turn untroubled
into sleep.

AUBADE

"I will not let you go". Our fears,
assembled in the old refrain,
move into morning. Shadows shake
the blades of leaves. Time's horses turn,
foamflecked upon the upper road.
Poised upon brightening, the sky
is suddenly a shout of birds
in apple trees. "And, dear, I die
as often as from thee. . . ." The words
have touched three hundred years or so
within your fingers on my cheek,
and, dear, I cannot let you go.

THE HAT

That crazy hat:
the first thing that I saw
of you that long-gone summer
was the hat,
blue, peaked, corduroy,
(I think from Paris),
but I guess you have
forgotten that

by now, as I should
have forgotten too,
should have forgotten
how we chattered, laughed,
and then, absurdly,
without meaning to,
looked in each others eyes
and knew, and knew.

EPISTEMOLOGY

Stranger than fiction
you say, kissing me,
to think of us together,
but it's true,
isn't it? I say
It is a story
older than the hills
yet always new
and perhaps not true at all;
we are a myth!
But myths are true, you urge,
all myths are true!
Truer than Truth, I whisper.
Truth's a lie
stranger than fiction
when I lie with you.

THE STATEMENT

If I say
that there is nothing between us

I am saying a thing
they will understand

as children understand
without enquiring

into the nature of nothing,
its endless cries

THE GIFT

I would send you
a rose, golden
and flared wide,
but there's no rose
wide and golden
enough to spell
out the sunlight
that I would send.

I would send you
a prayer, but all
those words are wooden;
their hasps rust.
I would send you
a ring, but rings
are meant for lovers,
and we are less.

Therefore I send
not rose, prayer, ring
but this which brings
what I would send.

YOUTH & AGE

*Old enough to be
your father!* Yes,
I play the cliché out
with wry surprise
at my anxiety
for her response,
but, with peculiar
brightness in her eyes,

she sits up straight
in our heat-crumpled bed,
then bends and kisses.
*Young enough to be
my child*, she whispers,
and, oh love, my lover!
moving upon me
ancient as the sea.

THE SECRET

Since love
without its secrets
pines and dies

as by-blows die
exposed upon
bare rock

to wind and night
and cold
and lurking wolf

I press
this primrose
in my pocketbook.

BY THE LAKE

Under our window
we may see
a beach, a boat,
a twisted tree,

and, far across
the shining lake,
a mountain changing
green to black

as wind scuds cloud
in from the West
and shakes the tree
to an unrest

that ripples water,
rocks the boat,
and sends the fingers
to your throat

in sudden fear
that this might be
the start of dark
for you and me.

SONG

The place she sleeps I know,
but cannot say with whom,
or even if alone,
or even if alone.

The way she smiles I know,
though cannot guess at whom,
or at her glass alone,
or at her glass alone.

COUNTRY SONG

I do not wish
to join this place,
its harbours humped
with rolling fish,
its orchards in a
hail of fruit
its cornfields duned
with swollen grain.

I do not wish
to meet the gaze
of smiling heavy-
bellied girls,
or push my own fist
in the tree
to pull the streeling
honey out.

Yet wishes are not
where I go,
for here, in spite of
thought, I think
the rippling muscle
of a back,
fruition's black
downfalling hair.

THE SAND IN THE OYSTER

If my love were in my arms
and if the night were long
what reason would I have to wrench
the silence into song?

INCONCLUSIVE

It is over, you tell me.
But is it over?

When it began we could
find no beginning,

sure of earlier lives
we must have shared,

how, therefore, can it end
that's had no ending

yet at any time,
but, cheating time,

met in each epitaph
the god descending?

THE DREAMER

It looks, she says, *so silly*,
leaning down,
mouth open, long hair
brushing at my thighs,
almost pathetic,
reaching out her tongue
softly to touch.
It dreams of Paradise,

I tell her, *poor, dumb,*
swollen-headed thing!
Her face is hidden
and her breath is hot
as then her mouth . . .
Or Hell, I whisper, *Hell!*
For Hell's the only
memory it has got.

AFTERWARDS

Forgive me,
but do not forget:
I know those words
we both have said
at parting,
but I also know
the chain of memory
bites the tree.

ON THE MOOR

I cannot quite remember
her eyes,
her mouth,

and that intensity
of shock
which hurled

hills trees walls
against the
rock of night

that sheltered us
until
re-ordered dawn.

I cannot, (quite),
remember
being young;

climbing,
the smell of heather
slows my footsteps.

THE CURIOUS

Reading these words
they'll ask me *Who?*
and I, my mind
on fire with you,
will smile, dissemble,
call them lies
who met them there
between your thighs.

THE RIVAL

No two men equally admit
the honey to the wine;
he offered you a clearer cup
than any draught of mine,

for I, with such a fury
of Paradise to share,
so thickened it with sweetness
as to choke you to despair.

IDENTITY

He must be he
and I be I
however desperately
you try
to think me him
or shape him me;
there's no escape
from constancy.

SUPPOSE

Suppose the moon,
and then suppose
beside the restless
hushing sea
our silence as
we pace the sand,
hand sharing hand;
suppose that we,

lost to all other
earth,confess
our secret solitudes,
expose
the nakedness
we bring to love,
the simple happiness;
suppose

that one of us
should then foresee
and fear the world's
censorious look —
then would the moon
and tide and sand
draw back and leave
but barren rock.

THE SEPARATION

Since it becomes us
to keep this
exact and difficult
space between us

for reasons given
and other reasons,
(so must the heart,
in trouble, hide),

I send you words
to make this space
itself a quality
of affection,

sharing with you
this distance that
enables messages
to be heard.

THE CAREFUL

Too cautious to say,
quite, *in love*,
we said we loved
each other, but . . .
We took each other
in the bed,
yet did not let
ourselves forget
the dangers of
that phrase, *in love*,
its power to bless
and wound and bind,
and so we loved
until in love
we found the hurt
that healed the mind.

THE WAKEFUL ONE

I will not sleep
though we have paid
our dues to love,
and long ago
you slid into
your deeps of dream,
for soon our nights
of love must flow

back into memory
and lose
through gradual time
their stolen light;
and so, awake,
I watch and hoard;
and so I will not
sleep tonight.

EROSION

The cliff crumbles;
the clay slides
down; my arm
around your waist,

I watch a brown sea.
Foam on foam
piles, ripples
a sour yeast

far beneath us;
the wind's whip
lashes the hair
across your eyes

red-brown as clay:
Hold tight ! Hold tight !
Or there's no shoring
in our lies.

THE INCREDULITY

I can't believe it —
kissing her mouth,
        a mouth so soft
        it would drown petals,
caressing her breasts,
        breasts firm

and delicate
    as a dream of music,
stroking her thighs,
    thighs warm
    and warm-gold
    as the dunes of summer,
meeting her hand,
    her young hand,
    gently enfolding
    my crowned sceptre,
    love-distended,
finding love
    asking for love —

I can't believe it.

THE REJECTION

No she said,
and tears were all her reasons.

Why? Why? Why? I countered,
unaware

that though Desire
may strip love's hunger bare,

if ruled by Love
it must obey Love's seasons.

THE PREDICAMENT

Bound together
with no hope of releasing
ever completely
heart or mind or hand,
held fast by unsaid vows,
unacted rituals,

trapped as the two halves
of a single mind,

we are agreed
upon the phrase "warm friendship",
agreed if this is love
it is friends' love,
and, careful not to pit
love against friendship,
sit long, talk long,
ignore the climbing wave.

RECURRENCE

Turning again
to themes of love,
the happiness
and the distress,

fumbling again
for words of love
to send my dear
and make all clear,

I find that love
demands again
that I pretend
love knows no end

though wanton love
will turn again
from her to her
should the wind stir.

CARELESS SPEECH

This happiness . . .
I say, and watch
a shadow move
across your eyes,

forbidding me
to end my words,
for love, it seems,
has made you wise

and given you
the power to know
that once such summaries
are said

the listening god
steals back the tide
of glory to its
ancient bed.

SPELL

Let in the clear,
let in the bright
that my love meet
her dream tonight.

Let in the smooth,
let in the warm
that sleep may keep
my love from harm.

Let in the moon,
let in the stars
to watch my love
through these still hours.

Let in the peace,
let in the peace
that all my love's
long sadness cease.

The Dialect

BEGGING THE DIALECT

for Christopher Hanson

The crumpled villages, guide-booked and mapped,
of a flat land by a flat sea, cold and wet,
make my destination, caul in hand,
begging from door to door the dialect.

*What is that? And that? And that? What did
your father call it? What his father? What?*
The thin quick ribboning of the sentences
whirrs to record the pause, the slur, the act.

Broken and blurred, pitched out of the one key
to turn the wards round and unlock a place,
I play it back. You notice, if you look,
the old men all have the one watching face,

hardened like cart-ruts in a hard frost, made
all the same ridge and hollow. PIaying back,
the lid reflects my darkly bended head
growing towards that sealed familiar mask

till I am asked, perhaps by my sons, *What
do you call that? call that?* The spool runs out.
Back again, I haunt them, caul in hand,
begging from door to door the dialect.

THE WORD

This worn-out word,
a battered bag
lumpy with protestations,
unguents, dreams,
shudders its slow bulk
interposed between
the frantic message
and the reaching arms.

What can one do with it?
How circumvent

the smell of hide,
the weight of lexicons?
Kicks break the foot or bury it.
Contemplation
heaves its maw apart
and spills out things

beyond prediction —
corners of dark rooms,
a rose bush by a gate,
a smear of lace
stuck to the monstrous skin,
a swollen breast,
larksong shrilling
above depths of grass.

It is unconquerable
and futile, muddling
crazed sobrieties
with rational games;
it is the treacherous
obstacle in which
we name the race, by which
we gauge the climb.

ARS POETICA

Learning
little by
little to
balance
pennies

on the rim
of an empty
ringing
wine-glass

while the
children
watch

is also
learning

little by
little to
talk to
listening

children

THE FENCE
for Tony Connor

Language, a peeling fence, cracks at the lean
of the silent creature we have always known
and patched with slats against, and nailed, and tied,
smelling through gaps the sweat that sours his hide,
and sometimes catching sight of hoof and horn.
They tell us wood is strong, that it has borne
his hard hurled shoulders from the very start,
though shaken still stands firm. Half-eased, we turn.
Behind us our own house is trampled down.

FLOWERS AND JAR

The attitudes of flowers and trees are strange
bright irresponsibilities of earth;
their leaf and blossom emphasize the spring's
alien language, far removed from love,
pain, or joy. Discover in the trees
the attitudes of green, but know them strange

to us and to our yearnings. In the spring
their gaiety is careless of the cold
bright steel of fear that threads our breath, and all
pain and joy of ours they do not know,
alien and apart. To think them kind
to us is lovers' fallacy each spring.

Indifferent years change. We, held in them,
alien to their rhythms, think the jar,
bright on our table, may control, conceal
their perfidies, but jars, as flowers, leave love,
pain, and joy aside, are not our mould,
indifferent as flowers; we see in them

the attitudes of green, but know them strange.
Pain or joy discover in the trees
alien language far removed from love;
their leaf and blossom emphasise the spring's
bright irresponsibilities of earth;
the attitudes of flowers and trees are strange.

THE PARKING LOT

My language thickening, I end the class,
hunching into my coat with modest smiles
at chattering gratitude. In the parking lot
my feet stamp echoes of revisions ruled
on student verses: here a soaring line
is blocked by one black adverb; here an image
slithers, crumples, falls. Nostalgia grips
my footprint like a chill. I shiver, warm
myself with memories. Those early stars
once patterned Plato and their harmonies rang.
Now stones upon the buildings crack with frost.
The parking notice staggers, drugged. The west
darkens and falters. Agonies ascend
into the ice, the spreading ice, the hands
reaching up from cold.

Virgil, return !
Teach me the circles of the human heart's
destruction of itself, for, order-makers,
masterless servants, we face emptying towers.
We are not young. We stamp cold feet. We drink.
We lie. We grow absurd, intent to claim
authorities we dreamed we had and dreamed
as falsely as our times.

The frost is keen
upon the parking lot. I back out, drive
through storms of student verses hellward home.

ANSWERING A QUESTION

Only to tell you why these structures are
is to disclose the only simple sun,
or maybe children playing hopscotch out
across the cracking pavements at their feet,
is to perplex with silence, or disturb
the haunted echoes of the dwindling barn
where great wheels turn to symbols, monoliths
hauled up to height across the land of straws,
is to make each word everything: but listen
not to the meanings but the spaces dropped
between the words. Sun. Children. Wheels. A Barn.
Only such telling spells us to ourselves.

Let's take the images. A man went out,
(let us pretend) into the day of sun
where children played. It could be any man
watching the cycle turn beginnings round
until the childish rituals shape their ends.
It could be any man. But this man went
slowly along to the deserted barn,
the red and yellow hay wains stabled there
beside each other, wooden beasts whose Troy
of towering haycocks to be razed and pulled
into imperial store still shivered green;

silent they were, and carved, like wooden gods.
And this man — well, what could he do or say
significant of truth — for truth's the thing
we're after, surely, in our unsure ways?
It seems evasion just to say he was,
but there he was, and here, still here, we are,
unanswerable figments, just as true
(or false perhaps) as how the image runs
its wayward hopscotch down the cracks in time,

as false or true as this that I have made
to tell you why these structures are their end.

It rests unanswered, after all, and all
we are precedes the question why we say.
I write this letter to make all things clear,
except that things are never clear as minds.
It could be any man. It could be you.
That any man is all the whys we are.
And why is one discovery, I suppose,
accepting questioning for what it is,
presenting how the questioning is itself
the perfect statement of the child that runs
from sunlight into the impending barn.

WHERE

I write this
without starting
down any track
but that of the words
making their spoor
towards somewhere
they at the end of it
can inhabit

and it is clear
to me in this
unwinding space
that as I drop
letter by letter
upon the page
this gradual message
I am stolen

away by my own
words procedure
from all that I
have supposed mine
and yours and ours

but where stolen
away to quite
remains in question

as the unrolling
paper ends
at its cut edge
and words go
on without any
smallest track

or sign into
extending air

THE NIGHT BEFORE THE LECTURE

In the wee small hours of the morning
I wrote this down:
Tell them that poetry, like life,
is an occasion
trapped by its own discovery;
tell them memories
shred in the hand like sand
as we learn our dying.

But do not stop there.
Tell them that life, like poetry,
is balanced upon precisions we never know
and rarely guess at —
walking the highest wire
oblivious to the gaze
of deaths and angels.

A New World

NEW BEDFORD

for John and Priscilla Hicks

I was born in the year
    the last whaler
left these wharves,
    and in earshot of the sea.
The old house groaned and creaked
    winds through the rafters
while I slept, hunched up
    in the hunting dark.
Impatiently the children
    tug my hands.

My Great Uncle Ted was a sailor!
    We troop along
Johnny Cake Hill. The empty
    seamen's Bethel
shines like wet skin in the rain.
    His widow
pecked out her saltless days
    between damp walls
webbed black with photographs.
    He was in sail.
That was before the steamships
    had really started.

The Museum gapes for us.
    Our family outing
clumps up wooden stairs.
    On every side
blue seas jet blood,
    harpoons thrust, boats are champed
to flinders. In the log
    a wooden stamp
thumps down each wallowing corpse
    that fed the lamps
with oils welled from the
    hacked meats of the sea.
My Grandad, your Great Grandfather,
    kept a lighthouse!
Did you know?

They watch the half-size whaler.
The Atlantic heard my
　　　Mother born.
Decks trust my feet.
　　　I go below. Brown ribs
curve round me. I am
　　　beating like its heart
and crouch a moment, carving bone,
　　　hunched, patient.
Gulls cry out like
　　　children high above.
Seas roar like streets.
　　　We are the last to leave
in hurrying rain.

Hold on. Hold my hand.

THE BRIDGE

*To the memory of Weldon Kees, whose car was found
abandoned on the approach to the Golden Gate Bridge,
San Francisco, July 18, 1955*

His car was found abandoned near the bridge.
That was the year my first book went on sale.
He was forty-one. Now, forty-one,
I cross the Delaware on Bethlehem Steel
riding Greyhound south to Washington.
I am tired. Some of my nerve has gone,

eaten away, discarded, no more use.
Stomped cigarettes shine from the travelling floor
flat messages. Indignities of hemlock,
offered no ease or patience, merely blur,
and shame remains a taste ; the paper cup
arranges flies where I have let it drop.

Ours is a small world without intimacy.
Deserts dissolve between the plate and plate
upon the table; spoons are open mouths
that cannot swallow; cups are frozen throats.
We stop off here to eat with blunted knives
as music spirals inwards, groove by groove,

unmanageable as history. Kierkegaard
lost out on marriage but pursued its doubt
and stained absurdity; I hunt for silence —
that is the only clue I haven't got,
and think at last permissible: the bridge
we cross upholds somewhere the crucial ledge

deliberately missed, the private place
where both directions lock above their fall,
expectant of our key. My frown finds stillness.
The good half of my face is stiff and sore
from ineffectual speech. Rejoin the bus?
I carry dying like a loneliness

kept secret and kept near, prepared for use.
Washington is white, sepulchural, bland.
The Library of Congress shelves his books
and mine together. It is time to end,
to finish talk, to learn a way to face
the golden bridge he climbed and did not cross.

THE RAKE

Half asleep, tonight I recall the poems.
Too personal, I said then. No-one should squint
at me, half smiling, knowingly, as they thumbed
those dangerous sheaves. Out there the darkness shakes
masks in the ivy — warriors that compete
with ghosts up from the pool, that pit of black
beyond the beds. A thing arm'd with a rake
gropes through my head. I must not look, will wake,
wake up, look round. The bookcase glass looks back —
well made, fine woman, threads of grey, the mouth
strong, yes strong, still strong. No-one got past.
And no-one does. Yet, stretching out these hands
clenched in my lap, observing how my breasts
round out the silk, my crossed legs bare one thigh's
unstockinged inches, womanhood remains
and warms me, as it always warmed me when
I started out to patronage, soft words,
those manly jibes — thought they could con a girl!

But pats on shoulders, even on the butt
were comeraderies I learned to share
while waiting for my chance. I knew my mind:
be docile first — (the lapdog has rewards) —
drink tea, admire, be helpful, candid, shy,
but lambent with intelligence. Make laughter
unforced, jovial. No-one got past.
Even he, with his millions, his flirtatious
little hints that warmed the rancid blood,
could not resist conspiracy; we shared
enthusiasms cosily until —
Gained access to the papers. Sheds new light.
Meticulous editing. No, none got past . . .
except, maybe, myself . . . *For Twenty Years*
the Leading Scholar in the Field . . . myself . . .
I snuffled through those papers till I blurred
as weariness blurs now. Impertinent fools
to doubt my stature! But no-one could break
that hedge of footnotes, no-one beat me to
the cache of manuscript. I knew the way:
cast doubt with kindness, condescending shrugs;
raise tolerant eyebrows; hint unsafe opinions;
talk of precedents — grow invulnerable
through discipline and art. If I'm alone
Who needs a man? Or poems? To join that gaggle
of poseuses who brag their weakness, sex,
and crass enthusiasms, girls like swine
rooting for lechery. Better to conform.
Professional. Decent tweeds. Plain skirts. A touch
of make-up only. Good shoes. Take a drink
but keep your distance. *Far too personal*
I said then....A thing arm'd with a rake
dragging up sentiment, those twisted shames,
those eaten sores. Damn follies for the fools
they turn us into! These loud ivy leaves
can clatter all they wish, the faces swim
up from the pool by hordes; who gives a damn
for ghosts, for childish ghosts! My face looks back
from book-case glass: fine woman and well made,
good teacher, scholar, dedicated, I
know what I am and teach. I teach the truth.
The Truth has mounted me. I bear His pride.

AT WALDEN POND

for David R. Clark

I stamp on the ice of a man a hundred years dead.
It holds. A pickerel fisherman draws blood
up from black water. Gingerly enough
I step out on the ice, my muscles stiff,
my world precarious as my reasons, and
in each one of my hands a child's gloved hand.

Memory should instruct us here. Ringed barks
of birch-clumps alternate their white with black,
their bronze with silver in crisp parchment rolls
My daughter slithers, stumbles, almost falls,
but doesn't cry. It's I that almost cry,
lumbered with children under this death-grey sky
a mile from Concord where the war began
and snowdrifts clog the bridge. They seem so young
to risk the ice, though it's more like to hold
their weight than my bear's tread. They can afford
the gestures I can't make, run far, and slide;
slowly we near the shore and the farther wood.

Memory strikes. I remember a school, a master
who soft-shoed his way after lights-out. Order
broke under his footfall. Stamps and jeers
surrounded him. I re-explore the cause.
Whose hunger, and whose guilt? The school was cold.
We hunted him like dogs through the blinding world.

Was that "Vox Populi" or "Demonstration"?
Disorder asks replacement by a name.
Armoured and starved, fish take a naked hook
and leap up to their death. The floorboards shook
in the red-walled dining room. The war
was novel still, and supper cocoa fumed
thin ardours to boy nostrils. He was blamed
as Emperors are blamed, or Governors, pitched
quivering upon anathema. I lurch.
My children scream half-laughters at the risk.

But I don't laugh. His heavy jewish face
blurred as a double image in the glass

of travelling windows has returned to chill
more than remembrance, and the running school
is suddenly upon the ice, a herd
stampeding through the failing light, some dead,
some twisted, from a war they didn't start
and couldn't end....I taste a dull cold hate
heading for Concord and far trees, my hands
held fast by children. Brooding, the hunter bends
above his lines. Red walls blur round the past,
and carefully we cross the darkening pond.

LINES FOR A LADY

E chi vedesse com' ella n' e gita,
Diria per certo: questa non ha vita.
　　　　　　　—CAVALCANTI

Remove your sleeping mask.
The drug is over.
Curtains heave to the slow push of the wind,
troubling their weighty flowers,
shifting rings
upon the long brown gleaming of the pole,
as dresden wriggles pastoral unquiet
on the death-cold marble beneath the mirror.

Shower now
in the ill-shaped converted bathroom
with the de Morgan tiles and the plastic curtain.
Adopt the face of the day
and gently sever
each retaining filament of evasion,
thus to accept the telegraph of the headlines,
the advertisements of destruction,
as a small
disquietude of elsewhere.
Death is listening
at the dead end of the telephone

you had disconnected for the night,
fearing the thin high voices,

the narrowing questions.
Re-connect now:
speech is frail by daylight;
fed by darkness, it is a different matter,
even a kind of nightmare,
the bodiless voices
tugging the pulse like elastic,
the one wrong voice
dragging the mouth down
at each sag of the curtain,
reminding cold of fingers smoothing the marble.
Now there is talk
like a cramped limb stretching the muscle,
easing and turning.

Dial, therefore, by memory.
It will ring.
The voice that answers will be harmless, light
in its understating renewals, its courteous rightness.
The heavy curtains are open on sliding rings,
and daylight stains your wrap;
there's nothing finished
by perfection, nothing the day won't stain
or the night escape.
      Make your appointment.
There is a message pad by the telephone.

DRUMBEAT

Far off in the night a drum
questions, shudders, and I turn
within the blanket, seeking dream,
as up above the lake the moon
confronts the astronaut with dusts
of the discarded desolate towns
that have no memory of their lodes.
I lay my pack upon a stone
as horsefly bite along the creek
and pray for gold. I press the key
and send my message, pulse on pulse,
through all the plenitude of stars

to someone at a grey machine
as gradual silence gathers round
the waiting moonscape and I stir
to sounds of rivers, wait to walk
unarmed and naked through the forest
there to find the only mask
that can possess me flesh and bone.
Far off, in the night, the drum. . . .

II

Jackpine. Brush. We crossed the border
that was no border and struck up
river until the river was no river
but a torrent drumming through the rock.
And then sage brush, grey-green, spinning
over the dry dust, sky hard
as the hard rim of the scorched pan,
river running blue and low,

and by the river raw earth
red and grey and white splayed
out on the hillside. Soon trees
and green reeds by wide lakes,
but now desert. I think desert.
I am the desert. A long day
towards endurance. Nights are cold.
I lie down on a cold star.

Beat the Drum.

Sparse trees. Poplar. Pine.
Our track the track of the fur trappers.
Sheer swamp. Black mud.
Beaver lodges build the lakes

by wide flats. And then the meeting
at the lake of the lost axe,
Chilcotin, Shuswap, Yubatan,
three tribes gathered for the games,

and we strangers, white-masked,
watching, waiting for the word.
Horses racing. Arrows flying.

Three days arguing peace or war,

and hard gambling. Some cheated,
the bone sleeved or half marked,
fires reddening dark faces,
and no hope of turning back.

Three days, then the word of peace.
The tall man pulls his trick,
shows gold, in his hand
a long journey on rough tracks

between jackpines, logs dropped
in corduroy across the swamps
to make the way, salt lakes
challenging our desire for water.

Feasting on deer, *Burn no bone.*
Call the coyote call. Revere
each live thing's need. And then the gold
at river's edge, the water clear.

Dance, dance, ankled by the deer.

III

Lonely is a crowded place,
a smell of earth, of tree-rot, fern,
loud sounds of tumbling water,
one leaf twitching in a wind
I cannot feel, a distant death
tremoring. The chipmunk jumps,
halts,skitters. Fire leaps
red, fills nostrils, waters eyes
as men crowd, women crowd,
forebears crowd, those worn names,
weathered masks. One sip of water.
Five berries. And my name?
I dare not ask. To ask is to
define and limit. I must wait.
A fern shivers. A leaf falls.
I do not sleep. I do not wake.

The shape begins. I tread a path
made by an older tread between
the sweating hemlock and the dark
and shuddering underbrush. A bird
alights. Is this the name? It flies.
I hear a bear. I smell a bear.
I have no knife. It knows and goes.
The chipmunk chatters. Is it here,
where sunlight leans a bar of gold
from pine-top to the moss-wet ground
that I am to be made my own?
Will there be vision?
       Vision comes,
face hot on mine, breath eating breath.
Named, I know and I am known.

Beat the Drum.

IV

Another space has altered time,
each step a leap, each careful breath
another minim on a dial
edging towards breathless death,
and every word recorded, fixed
in pulse and cadence, every pause
and action trapped. I stare through glass.
The Earth is very old and far
and blurred and small. The desert waits.
I put my boot into the dust
of every myth from then till now.
Machinery hums. The voices burst
in loud, then crack and falter, fade.
I am the man upon the moon.
Gloves grope at rock. I pick a chip.
It glistens like the heavy gold
and could be deadly. Is it dead?
Alive or dead, it has no name.
I sweat within the helmet mask.
I take one step and soar like fame
beyond the sensible. I stop.
Go careful. Slow. The voices call.

The image is not sharp. Adjust
the lens, the dial. Ten more breaths.
Receiving you. The needle shifts.
I am inaccurate as time
has proved itself upon this plain.
I (rasp) climb (thud) the ladder (bone
grown heavy) sleep. The pulses drum.

V

Found !
          At the moment of finding
a leap of the heart,
a break in the pulse :
                    in that moment
the mask looks back,
marked with the moment,
gold eyes in the mask,
dusts of the endless desert on the skin,
a sudden glory.
                I turn back
to cards and firelight, reason dead
and passion blazing.
                    I return
to carve the mask that grips my head
with history and the dance.
                        I hurl
to splash-down in a smoking sea,
discovery trapped.
                They watch, applaud,
as if some immortality
shone from the nugget, mask, and stone,
and not the death for which we came,
as if all moments were not one
unchanging moment changing names
as creek as forest and as moon;
light hides within a changeless form
accepting every change we name.

Dance. Dance. Dance. And beat the Drum.

THE INSCRIPTION

The dead girl
wrote to the
poet when she was
alive

and he was
alive and gave him
her poems that
lie

here on the
shelf now he is
dead and her
dead

voice saying
thank you is
no one talking to
no one

THIS FRIDAY, FLYING WESTWARD

Drunk above North Dakota, stoned out of my mind,
I've nothing but my smile and a bourbon wobbling
round in the glass, slip-slop, and a nice plain guy
en route to Viet Nam called Cohn, who's never been
this far from home before. The distance slides
below and round, round, round . . . dimension grows
delusory, my memory choked with cloud
and skidding geometries of field . . . night drifting
slowly down . . . tree-frogs, their throats patched white,
antiphonal, loud . . . the flavour rich . . . then silence
shifting into high. . . .
        Now high, high, high,
I talk to Cohn. His tongue crawls like a fly
across the space to say *I'm scared,* but says
*Parachutist. Meant to get to school
but waited for the bread. Took too damn long.*

243

Caught by the draft. Inadequacies throng
moralities too tender to be borne
as, pinnacled, I watch the gargoyle frown
jut from his collar, wince, crane, gape, and look
down, out across Dakota. I tell him snow
comes next on higher peaks, perpetual cold,
eternal. . . . His eyes dull. He slumps and snores
within a private place, encapsuled, quaint,
defenceless. Ash extends my cigarette.
Dakota slides like cards across the boards
of a bar-room brawl. Six-guns are out
as tables fall. Who sees God's face must die
as light dies in the mind . . . limbs gangling, toppling,
crumpling to the big sound of the spin
and certitude of stars — those whirling spheres
we trapped in fingers, pampered, and let go
to pattern their fatalities, unloosed
by diamonds and the strike of time. . . .
                          Below
the wrinkling alters. *Have another drink?*
I nod, nod, nod. The world is nodding off
into its dream of ease, gun in its hand . . .
green thoughts...green thoughts...tree-frogs,
their throats patched white
loud as this pulling lung...the arbour warm...
alone in Paradise...alone...alone...
and high, high above bare North Dakota
and that wrinkled skin, those shuddering clays,
I choke again on cloud...my fingers clutch...
We gasp through gardens on our buckling knees.

A SLICE OF LEMON
For Bonamy Dobrée

A slice of lemon in my tea,
a sun
made by the pale crayon in the drawing
whose colours outrun uniforms,
whose smiles
extend beyond the faces of their rhymes:

there colours spill out; scribbled
free and red,
the mouth escapes the face as if it knew
the passion to transgress,
or how to fit
its clownishness to every passing kiss,

like kissing metals on a black
wet road
the hollow hour between breath and breath
when nothing makes its pass;
at three o'clock
the phone: crashed head-on and a total loss.

At Belle Fourche, South Dakota,
the huge hearse
took us from the automobile graveyard
down to the wide street's haze;
"Hell of a hearse,"
the man said in the back, "No Goddam ash-trays !"

A slice of lemon in my cup,
a moon
slit from the sour round of those moral tales
that brought rags riches;
foolishness is dead,
red silks of blood under November hedges.

A slice of lemon souring up
the mouth;
her skin was greasy and coarse, her jawbone long,
her lipstick the wrong tone;
amendment died
in the dust-clogged grass of a badly cambered lane.

"Hell of a hearse," the man said
at Belle Fourche,
"No Goddam ash-trays," fingering the velvet,
the dusty ebony, the brass.
We drove
along Fifth Avenue on one of those

surrendered empty mornings when
the sun
is lemon yellow, shadows sharp and long,
and memory unvexed as the sky;
it seemed
if we had anything we had the time. . . .

A tartness on the mouth,
a yellow sun,
a lemon yellow moon, spin in her cup
whose eyes are blind as fur,
whose blood has run
dark through the stiffening dusts to which we turn

in time, from time. "Hell of a hearse,"
he said.
We rode Fifth Avenue to the store, and felt
like Lazarus. We lived,
whoever died.
I pin this on her leaden coverlid.

A POET AT FIFTY

April remainders me upon this green
and white-faced campus, spilling girls —
long-legged, blonde-haired, pout-breasted — out in droves
of teal-blue hipsters, paisley skimmers, fishnets,
poorboys, bronzine slims, tights, boots. Books flash
bold titlings. Folders, hugged to bellies, slide
Spring light off tilting planes. A plump dark man,
grey hair thick at the nape, bags under eyes,
bush-bearded, in my crumpled bawneen, I
steer blind through dazzle, sirred and smiled, my tongue
thick with its difficulties. Even at fifty,
gasping chalk smoke, watching faces — apples
laid in rows, with raisin eyes, straw-haired —
obsessed with accuracy and chance, I labour
over these tensions, these defeats, though silence,
thickening, thickens every skin until,
trapped in a leprosarium, fumble-thumbed,
stump-footed, leonine, I mouth spit and turn

beast again, hump, rut, sweat bourbon, blink
back drowning veins, blurred visions, to be man
still in that way, reminding man of man,
love in a special sense. I sense my time
one of occasions and of failures, crouch
behind shame, scribbling, ash upon my coat
fall-out of talk for gales of plaudits, *Now
here is Our Visiting Poet.* Those masks of dough
flabby with information. And the wives.
Oh God, the wives! — And smiling men in collars
talking Proust, hands moist upon the glass.
This, for all that reputation seeks,
remains the guerdon. Autographing books,
I forge convictions of a labelling name
still in the business, on the scene — Reviews,
Recordings, Broadcasts, Lectures — even poems
cropped cautiously, infrequently displayed.
*Work of the Last Ten Years. Such Rigour, Ease,
and Mastery.* My second wife said *Master? —
Master Bastard!* Wrote upon her back
that night, still in her, crazy. Then the kids...
Sometimes a letter, now, from a college room,
beginning *Father*....Father of lies, whose lies
are so like truth they're true, whole books of true
and inescapable truths, my mind its truth,
no falsehood possible. Except desire.

POEM ENDING WITH A LINE BY THOMAS KINSELLA

Grading his paper, I see him standing
knee-deep in jungle, waiting to be shot,
stupid and likeable as ever. Rings
around misnomers and innaccurate facts
gash craters in the page. Wrecked sonnets rust
and pastorals crumble; ants march through the waste
in scuttling columns, clambering leaves; the dawn
sweats out its dues on Pegasus torn down;
and I write *Superficial, Incomplete,*
which is,in fact the case. He held his seat
through lectures like a cat upon a horse,

all four limbs stiff, eyes nervous, waiting for
the moment he could jump. He's jumping now,
down to gunfire, sweating, and around
his bloated parachute the final stars
remain mysterious. He confuses Mars
with Menelaus (wrongly spelt): Too bad!
That sin against the language kills him dead.
I have to save it from him, send him down
flat, slap, on jungle mud, his lungs aflame
with breathlessness, his eyeballs harsh with sweat.
The gods are wheezing slowly to their feet
and, poised to draft him, only wait for this
last comment: *Failed.* I'm signing his release
from everything he doesn't know he knows
and cannot spell. Ink stains my hand. Suppose
I let him pass? What then? Can Truth brook schism?
In certain cases death is a criticism.

THE FRIDAY FISH
for Percy Jarrett

We lived ramshackle that summer in a cabin
toppling onto the shore; a big madrona,
red-skinned, smooth-limbed, curved the stiff horizon
that returned our gaze through age-smeared windows;
the nearby headland held in clumsy brush
the cabins and wrecked cars of the Reservation.

It was Friday. We'd let the dinghy lie
awash all week to swell the planks. The tide
had drowned the barnacled rocks, the spitting clam-bed,
and wriggled at the shingle. We dragged her down,
keel rasping pebbles, pushed her off, and jumped.
Our tackle rattled. We would jig for cod.

Smoke rose in grey ropes from the Reservation
where nobody moved ; the water slid,
unwrinkled, dark; the sun blurred, faltered, bloomed
soft crimson, the horizon smeared with blood.
But we were in the shadow of the land,
and only our faces altered, flushed and carved

by patience and the sun's death. Up and down
the tips of our rods moved — then something bit:
you struck, reeled in; the trace was bitten through.

That was the way it went for perhaps an hour.
Figures came out of the cabin, waved their questions
under the madrona. Children cried
excitements of expectation thin as loss.
But all the traces broke. The sea grew darker.
The sky was flushed. Winds chilled us from the West.

A wire trace, I said. *We'll fix the bastards!*
A wire trace it was: we gently knocked
our leads upon the bottom, reeled in some inches,
lifted, and let fall, kept patient rhythm,
gazing off at lengthening swallowing shadows.
Most of the Reservation had turned black.

And then it bit. I struck, reeled in. At first
it was a dream in the water, a swerve of meaning
greenly transient, then a slap and flash
of exclamation at the side of the boat,
diving, dragging down, then back, then up
slowly to suddenly kick. Too late. The net
scooped up: it thrashed between our drowning feet.
I took the club and killed. Once. Twice. Again.
The sky was watery blood. I split the skull.

Rowing back, the questions came over the water.
"Dogfish — three foot, maybe!" "Dogfish?" "Yes."
Stubborn to gain from murder, I refused
distaste and doubt, upon the beached log laid
the long corpse out, picked up the knife, and at
the first brush of the blade it curved and jerked
in jacknife, and its jaw snapped, plap! You dropped
the rag. *"It's dead,"* I said. *"Just nerves. Don't fret."*
"Dead?" you said. *"Quite dead!"* The knife was not
half sharp enough; the wet skin rasped our hands;
the scales were chips of mica, splinter-thin;
but, heaving from the elbow, I at last
ripped up the belly, and the spill of gut
slopped out in red and silver blotched with black,

looped, sagged, and squirming. Using both my hands
I grappled it, and threw. You turned aside
uneasily. Then, three yards out to sea,
we saw the stomach sac, still round, float up
and, in its glistening, five small black fish
still blindly swimming, prisoners.
        "They're alive!"
you said. We could not move. The slippery knife
was rigid in my hand. And *"Let them out!"*
you cried, too late.
        The tide was black. The waves
bore them into the vast unravelling dark
we shuddered at, as, heaving up our catch,
we climbed the track beneath the black madrona,
turning at the top, horizon gone,
the Reservation fathomless in gloom.

HISTORY

In Memoriam, J.F.Kennedy

I am a monster.
Among small
crouching years,
I take up

Death in my hand
and Death shakes
wild as a shrew.
I pile bones

high by the wall.
I eat graves.
Chanting,
they bring me
graves to eat.

A BAD DAY THROUGH THE BERKSHIRES

for John and Priscilla Hicks

A bad day; the kids jabbing
screams at my nerves; the Mohawk trail
slowly unwound past curtaining ice
on flanking rock-slabs
through leaf-brown cleaved hills.
A bad day: time left me
alone there under a dull sky
clicking my shutter;
the car, hauled
to a green standstill by the bridge,
waited.   I clicked.   *Keep this,*
the camera commanded.   *Keep this.*
Things are important.   Rocks, trees,
foams of water.   A man's eye
watches, records.   A woman holds
children warm as the snow piles
higher, higher.   I fear death.
A stone shakes in the stream's flow.

I stand on a stone and teeter, crazy
to make my picture.   Foam spills
foam at my feet.   Clouds herd
clouds round the November sun.
And colour dies.   A dark shutter
remains dark in my nerveless hand.

Pioneer Valley. Call it the journal
of yet another day lost out
to an obsession. The kids cry
for games and candies. My wife sees
a leafless tree with yellow apples
crowding the twigs.
Should I take that?

The sky's too grey.   The tree stands
close to buildings.   Wires track
from pole to pole across the twigs,
civilized beyond all hope.

My son sees cows. He likes cows.
When we reach Williamstown we eat.

A bad day. The kids ate,
messily, nothing.   In white rooms
Degas, Renoir.   Perfected flesh.
My daughter, heavy on my shoulders,
calls a naked bather *Mum,*
likes a bronze horse. I hump symbols
among symbols, my dark eye
dark in the bad light.
          Evening falls
like a man from a bridge in slow motion
on all our screens in all our homes.

GHOST SHIRTS
In Memoriam, Theodore Roethke

Wovoka believed
in a Messiah,
a newcomer,
the plains black
with buffalo,
taught the tribes to dance,
tell the truth,
not fear death,
and gave them shirts.
This morning shirts
arrive for me
from a dead poet.

Imagination
evolves deaths.
They sang through bullets,
boys in rain
catching the wet in their
mouths, licking
their bare arms.
The shirts fit;
the same shoulders,
the same neck:

I stare out from
his photograph.

The consequences
of prophecy matter
less than the act.
At Wounded Knee
that Christmas time
two hundred died;
for thirty days
the Ghost Dance War
choked up the trails.
The Gods allow
us transformations
the earth foils.

I wear a dead poet's
shirt. Belief
derides the ring of
firelit faces,
as all history;
in Nevada
the prophet,
every victory won,
praised as I praise
the dead that dance
the dance, are truthful,
and consume.

ONE MORNING

Red curtains move.
Deliberate fingers plug
in harder and pull back.
The weight of blood
resists with sag and fold
but parts at last
upon a glare of white
whose altered planes
include no footprint.

Boughs about to crack
have lost distinctness
upon pewter cloud.

Warmth of the huddled house
weeps down the glass
as cups tap cymbals
under plumes of steam
and linens fumble.
Now we break the fast
imposed by darkness
and look out upon
astonishments of white.
The commonest roof
has made a shift
and settled into sky.

Before us lies the sea,
an endless bruise,
its scarcely moving skin
unwrinkled, flat,
expressionless, a soiled
long-wearied thing
that field and hill usurp
this dawn to act
out roles of pity,
terror, light. We clap
like birthday children
trusting gods of snow.

NIGHT POEM, VANCOUVER ISLAND

I

The wind's in the west tonight,
heavy with tidal sound;
the hush and rattle of trees,
the indrawn breath of the shore,
do what they must; waves slap
at the tip and stagger of stones,
and the night tonight is black;

blackness without intent
moves over the globe
as waters move. The shoals
are nosing into the storm.

Blackness moves over the globe.
Will this wind never drop?
The house, awash with air,
swings into the dark,
and, all its lamps ablaze,
challenges time and fear.
I see a wall of ice.
Newspapers fall like flowers.

Turn in the bed, my Love.
Reach out. We almost touch
but, swimmers pulled apart
by arbitrary tides,
are swept out on the night.
Somewhere a hand will find
that delicacy of bone
locked in a glacial year.
We label history now.
Fossils, our smiles extend
the frontiers of the past.
Our kisses breed new terms.

The sea speaks as it must.
We lie together in
a hollow of the sound,
clasped hands entangling bones.
We have our prayers to say.
We have our seed to spend.
We half believe in day.

Sleep is difficult now.
Loudly the pump of the heart
and the rasp of sheet on sheet
answer voice with voice.
Turn in the bed, my Love.
We were a distant tribe
that died. These waters move
the history from our bones.

II

Darkness begins and ends
all that we have and are;
stilled in this night of gale
on the long death of a bed
I reconstruct such lives.
I hear the forest birds
scream over the shore.
I watch the slide of light.
Does history begin?
Feet beat upon bare earth.
Whales rise in the sea.

Something created here:
logic travelled moss
upon the hospitable boles
and lichen dribbled song
from boughs the bines make laws.
Walking to rules of boughs,
listening to wings in the pulse
and breakers over the heart,
I become stone. I pause
to accept the tread of the sun
and the worm under my cold.
Clay is part of me. Grass
patterns me; meshed in rain
by grass, I stare like a toad.
Prayers rot on me like fern.

Do not touch me. Look,
but do not touch. My smile
has red meat in its teeth.
My skin is soft with fur,
and I am wiser than dogs.
Your mouth upon my mouth,
your freed persuasive breasts
could end a different tale
but are irrelevant here.
Press close. Your V of hairs
and buttery mandible nip
most freedoms in the bud,
and your haunches ride

the nightmare to its knees,
but I am not the night,
or free, or beast, or king.
I have no dark or bed.

    Light slid up to the shore
here from the stiff sea.
Trees were huge with rain
and the square teeth of bears.
Eagles reach their wings
out above whales; head down,
a toad stood on the lip
of speech and sang its flies.

    I am afraid. The hunter
only obeys the laws
of chastity and death.
I do not know his code
that changes as herds grow
or lessen, hungers change.
The salmon leap up through
the membrane. Narrowing hills
shudder, contract, and grip
all they can get. The gun
is levelled, the bow drawn.
Time has its lives to eat.

III

    Abandon me. I am lost
in the sweat of my own dark.
Rivers include my eyes.
Forests evolve my hands.
Over the valley hawks
gather into the eye,
watching the movements of death.
I am a name for the sea.

    Leave me. Let me be.
Somewhere the ships turn home,
the animals bless the sun,
the thundering lungs fall still,

and the stone eyes smile.
Something created me
because of that one place.
I wear it round my bones.

Who is a wooden mask
painted with teeth. I stood
alone on the island for days
until a whale spoke out.
Its eye was a bead of blood,
its fin curved as an adze,
and its head a hill.
Who is an ivory jaw,
a black glistening skin,
a boat floating alone.

How is a scar on a rib.
I have forgotten craft
and practice. Knives obey
orders I cannot give,
having no rules or words.
Fish come to my hand.
How is a crooked bone,
a bird dropped on the wing.

Why is not my business.
Causes are different worlds.

IV

I am the sound you make.
Leaf, twig and stone
compose me like a song.
I am the inch you crawl
closer, lifting the bow.
I am the lens of air
through which the hunted move.
We are creation's kind.
Look out! An eagle falls
in every seed we spit.

Fish jump in every thumb.
We are destruction's kin.
Be still. A heron soars
in each astonished breath.

V

Something created here
the lives time has to eat.
Something invented time,
a wrinkle upon the sea.

Only the dead awake.
The living have no need.
Lapped in a fold of water
travelled across the globe
to end up finally here,
I lift up my arms,
but not to Death. I kneel
but not to Love. I hold
existence close, not beast,
or god, or man, but breath,
more simple and less sure.

Come now, if you wish.
The wind from the west has stilled.
Your mouth upon my mouth
solves nothing but is good.
Light rises from the sea
and time spreads with the light.
Put your body to mine;
we are the world we caused.

Amores

THE FORGIVENESS

I have remembered
what is going to happen,
your withdrawn boots
collapsed beside a chair,
your dress dropped at the bedside,
your bare breasts,
as, in the hall, you pat
your mirrored hair,

draw on your gloves,
thank me, and thank my wife,
calling your husband
from his golf-club grin
at someone indistinct,
today concluding
all those pleasures
our tomorrows bring

as they repeat their history
in the heat
of mutual nakedness.
I play my part
So nice to meet you!
Glad that you could come!
forgiving you this ending
from the start.

THE LOYALTIES

Though we are loyal
(you to him
and I to her) ,
resolved upon decorum;
though we are cautious
(I of her
and you of him),
intent upon discretion,

nevertheless at meeting
(you with him
and I with her)
we always court disaster,

kissing so lightly
and so quickly that
all shrewd observers
must suspect us lovers.

A DREAM OF DROWNING

He has set spies upon your door;
your dry lips flutter in their sleep,
shadows drag across your brow
your dream twists down ; ship's cages, cracked
upon the rocks, heel as you drop
down further shelves through greener dusks;
my hand is heavy where to ask
acceptance now would storm your drowned
grief down across my cradling chest.

Did faithless Deirdre die for this?
Eyed like a ewe between two rams,
she parted lips, closed blue-lid eyes,
and kissed rock she was driven on
because the sweet hair in her groin
was laid out for another man's
enormity of casual taste;
have you that chain about your waist?
I kiss your shoulder and your hair
sways in the dark remembered past.

I stare through deeps. A sailor drowned
in orange weed swings out across
your journey in a wild embrace
of wide-flung arms; your fingers brush
the trailing fingers of the world's
descending visions: I escape
the meshes of that murderous sleep
and slide from bed. You do not stir.
The huge moon drifts me up and up.

THE LEAF

Taste! you said.
I tasted.
The leaf was bitter,
but as a spice is bitter,
the aftertaste
sharpening my breath
all afternoon,
even changing the sense
of the words I placed

so carefully,
and would have tinged each kiss,
had kisses not been cancelled
for the day,
he strolling watchful
under other trees
and you, eyes lowered,
eager to betray

no hint of that communion,
how my lips
taking the green leaf wafer from your hand
had reverently pressed
the fingers, how
we hungered, how
the spices drenched the land.

THE ALTERATION

So cold, so cold?
I dare not ask
the reason, for
what reason's there
is minded like
the tide, the moon,
the hidden running
of the river,

not like man,
that, thrust apart,
reviews the riddles
in his store,
believing that
some trick of phrase
can change the season
and the hour.

THE RESOLUTION

Though writhing nightly
in my bed, protesting
desperate love, she still
repeats her firm
resolve to end it
from the highest motives,
always from the very
highest motives,
truth, integrity,
her absent husband,
and her shame, her planned
assenting shame.

DUODECORUM

I
This poem is to a person.
I make poems
as others love.
        I give you
from this shore
whatever shoals, rocks, shells, tides
shake the sense,
all falling, lifting, sliding, thrusting down
of feet on dunes,
and catalogue the nerves
that run beneath the sands
like roots of trees

to someday tip the world:
each place I look
you lie down in my light;
though storms peer back
I see them.
   They are yours.
You will not drown.

II

Do you remember?
We shook hands,

and our hands knew
they would share bed

right from that greeting.
You put on

your gloves again
with surprised eyes

and talk faltered.
Your breasts, firm

within their comforts,
refused belief;

your flanks doubted:
over wine

our hands brushed,
and our hands held.

III

We said,
   "Let us be clear
that all we do
is gentle, hideous, strange,
that the tidal tug
is common to sea and test-tube
as to blood

266

and what we figure by blood,
and that we know
we are saying yes to the ruthless
ridiculous power
that breeds the fly from the dung,
the dung from the flower,"

and,
        "Let us be sure
from the very beginning of this
lonely affair in the darkness
that we sign
our names to the blood on the stone,
to the grin of the dog,
and that there is little hope
we shall learn to forgive
even our own discoveries.
much less failures.
Darkness rewards its own,
but we are creatures
partly absurd with light.
Let us begin
with a prayer that we may be granted
one ignorant kiss,
and that we may, in that moment,
venture kindness."

IV

You stripped without watching.
There was no
reason to watch me.
I had come
entirely for this;
my male presence
completed the shape
of the night air,

and I, suddenly
stilled, appalled
at the ease with which
I had become

267

agent and avatar,
felt cold
at the rise of the flesh
to such inward furies.

V

Adultery.

This
is the word hissed
by the shifting sheet.
I turn over,

having accomplished
something,
      a schoolboy
sharpening his truth
on a bold lie,

then lean on my elbow,
stare down.
Your face is a sorrow
of used skin

and carved human.
The mouth spoils.
Alone as Pyrrhus,
I damn Plato.

VI

Person to Person....
It is this
that dignifies
the peculiar hurt,
the sagging wound.
I say your name.
You murmur mine.
The pain endures.

VII

I send you happiness,
the shape of an apple
upon brown wood,
the fall of water
through sounds of trees,
a child's arms
warm round the neck,
a quiet summer.

I send you this
as recompense
for the wounds you have opened,
the black roots

you have planted deep,
the dark gifts
I have gained at your hands
that promised riches.

VIII

We meet again.
But there is a skin on the sun.

Something has coated our eyes
and thickened our hands.

Mute, we stare at each other,
two carved gods

whose rituals have uncovered
brutal conquerors.

IX

Person to person,
                    I said.
Wrong!

It is river to river.
the fish rise

through swollen waters.
The failing light

fuses the trees.
The blood comes.

X

Absence defines us.
There are others.
None with my hands.
Your mouth is small

under their mouths.
Your heavy flanks
move in your skirt.
There is no moon,

no faith, no hesitance.
It matters
little to seas
where the seas go.

I drown, swimming.
I say "swimming"
knowing that grip
has tidal claws.

XI

"Well," you may say,
"it is all over:
a day and a night
and a man gone
away skyward,
a far country."
"Well," you may say,
"it is over, done,
finished, completed..."
Nothing completes
itself in this
enormous world

of search and hide:
no name remains
rock in the teeth
of the blowing sand.

XII

To whom am I writing?
There is no language to say.

I walk down the road to the store
with my head full of people

and every one of them you
as you are everyone

remote in the desert
combing your long black hair.

ACCURSED

Every time your name
crops up at work,
I can't help it
suddenly I'm wet!
She stares, huge eyed,
across the café table.
The skin is flushed and taut.

And just your name —
not even touching you!
Her lip is trembling.
Tears are in her eyes.
Damn you, she mutters, *Damn you!*
and her hand
upon my hand is hard
and cold as ice.

THE HEMISPHERES

She rinsed her mouth.
I watched the water spin
away in spiral :
on her narrow chest
the dark-ringed nipples spun;
her navel spun:
drunk, I told her
That could be a test
for which half of the globe
we've done it in
Northside it's clockwise,
but Southside reversed!
She pulled her panties on.
So what! she said,
and, fumbling, I
attempted to rehearse
that hazy formula,
the cosmic sign
that might interpret
all our crazy game ;
North right, South left
I mumbled, and she smiled,
cupping her brassiere
to twin points of flame.

THE EVIDENCE

Explain this! I am ordered.
She has found
upon the flyleaf
of a book of verse
picked up for pennies
certain words addressed
in my own hand
but to a name not hers
although the date is recent
and the joy
commemorated happened
in her reign.

Explain! she says
and means *Explain away!*
I say, "But there is
nothing to explain.

It was a simple, candid
act of love —
that love you taught me
long before we met,
even before your birth —
Love's love of love!
How is it possible
you could forget?"

WAITING FOR A LETTER

Tomorrow I may hear.
Of course!
But till tomorrow
I am caught
between the wish
to send you love
and that to ban
such dangerous thought,

being aware,
(as are we both),
of love's absurdity,
its greed,
its tyranny,
and, too, unsure
that love's what either
of us need,

yet being also
most aware
that for a little while
we two
released that great
imprisoned prince

and found what love
revealed may do,

and found, moreover,
that the text
within love's book
is falsely glossed,
for lovers also
may be friends
and prize affection
over lust.

APHRODITE PANDEMOS

"The first time's never good
with me," she said. "I turn
on slowly." I caressed
her crotch without alarm
and kissed a nipple. This
could be a form of bliss,
to know all that could come
of it was private ease.

"I like it lots, of course,"
she told me. "I don't make
love just to raise my score
in bed with one more man.
I think that sex is fun,
but — please don't get me wrong —
tonight I'm pleasing you:
I mean there's always one
that wants it more and one
that wants it less, but gets
a kind of minor kick."
She kissed me hard. She said,
"Don't be upset. I don't
mean I'm a ruddy saint:
I knew soon as we met
that we'd end up in bed.
But now that we are here —
just think I am a whore.

I'll make it really good."
She made it good. She said
"Was that what you'd in mind?"
She rubbed up very close.
She said, "I go for this.
Not being quite turned on

is good, you know, sometimes,
I mean it's kind of good
to do it for itself
and give a man his kicks —
I mean it's like a friend —
we don't have to pretend.
Love's great, but it's a mess."

I slept moralities.

THE TRIUMPH

It's not too much to say
I am delighted
to find you once lay
in that bastard's arms,
giving him what you now
give me, exciting
him with those delicate fingers,
insistent charms.

Such pleasure, you will tell me,
is perverse.
It is absurd
to think of him; so many
years have passed
you scarce recall his face;
besides, he was a passing
fling, not any

heart-pierced Grand Romance,
and long dismissed,

quite meaningless!
Have you no understanding?
Here in your bed
that pig's at last a ghost,
displaced, defeated,
and I crowned, upstanding!

THE FRIENDS

I took off my suit
and she her dress
and we both slid
into the narrow bed.
It was near dawn;
we'd talked the whole night through
and were assured of being,
as we'd said,

friends, but no more than friends.
No problem here.
We needed sleep.
There was one bed. And so
we lay down
merely neighbours for the night,
cramped by necessity,
but sleep came slow

and we were restless
though we both lay still.
Then suddenly she tugged
her panties down
and turned to me
with soft enquiring hand
and found my candour
equal to her own,

my loneliness as great,
my need the same.
We fucked and then we slept.
The wordless dawn
half woke me and I touched

her head and knew
unasked and somewhere else
a child was born.

PRECIPICE

Her leather coat
shone in the sun. She threw
one booted leg across
the other, lit
a cigarette, leaned back.
The leather creaked.
She said, "I bet
you'd have a bloody fit

if I said that I'm very
good in bed
and really fancy
doing it with you!"
I sat upon the terrace edge.
I said,
"I'm really not quite certain
what I'd do —

but I am sure I wouldn't
have a fit."
Below the parapet
the cliff dropped sheer
in hacked confusion to the sea.
I said,
"I might leap at the chance
or, perhaps, off here!"

and smiled at her.
She shuddered and smiled back.
"It's bright outside," she said,
"but still too cold
to sit out long. Can we
go in the house?"
I said, "The Spring
is only three days old —

we mustn't be impatient !"
At the door
she turned and laid
one black precarious glove
against my cheek. She muttered,
"Spring is Hell
if you are good in bed
but bad at love !"

THE RETURN

All winter I
have had that room
inside my head,
the gas fire's hiss,
the ragged rug,
the naked girl,
and every night
returned to this

perpetual question:
Will it be
the same, the fire,
the rug be there?
And she, her white slip
struggled off
above her dark head,
then her bare

warm body in
between the sheets?
Can two rooms ever
be the same —
that one remembered
long and lost,
and this I walk to
through the rain?

ASHAMED

You were ashamed
of the soft down on your bottom,
I of my member's
huge-bulbed gracelessness :
delicately I caressed
that delicate bottom;
graciously you rewarded
gracelessness.

Never were two more suited,
each one's shame
answered with, first, affection,
then desire :
now I lie sleepless
dwelling on your shame,
and shamelessly desiring
your desire.

IN JULY

Writing this naked,
or near naked
(your ring on my finger),
in the airless house
of high summer,
gnat-stung,
and stung by the memory
of your kiss

I itch, scratch,
nails and words
raking at skin
and spirit both,
and find once more
there is no balm
for a summer gnat
or a woman's truth.

At The Centre

AT THE CENTRE

When you can say *Long Ago* of your own memories
you have arrived at the centre.
                      Walking the plaza,
a face in a window stares, half-blurred, half-vivid,
and in your reflection shapes and colours
cancel half the cheek, define the brow
perhaps with a plastic bucket, an Indian sweater
black with emblems, or perhaps with shadow.

Familiar recognition presents its muddled
combination of fantasy and distortion:
long ago a girl said something gentle
about that dragged-down mouth, those hooded eyes,
under a wartime sky whose blues were sharper
than the colours of toys and no less tempting,
but it was all a dream, a girl in a window
making impossible gestures with plaster arms
to wrench the cotton right, and a masculine dummy
with a superman jaw and joy-boy eyes.

Now, however, passing another window
the plaster faces travel through your own
varying countenance, and are assignations,
idiocies, perfections long ago
completed and found wanting.
                            Windows flash
bland appetites;
              there's softness at the centre.

SOLO

I am supported in my conviction
by twenty years of that conviction,

every failure justified
by twenty years of equal failure.

Obstinate ways, you say, provide
proof of nothing but obstinate ways:

habit, like mastery, is a truth
particular to each man as skin.

POEM ON HIS THIRTY-FIFTH BIRTHDAY

Halfway to where God only knows,
is it a trick like the ant's scuttle,
this all-for-Art, this home-making,
to end on the tip, a used bottle?

All's made in belief that what stays
somewhere around when boxed down
is more than a smell of old cheese,
a torn postcard flushed down the drain,

but is it more? Bones of my father
in me maybe, but his own creaking,
stiffening, soon rid of. A good Dad
in terms of a good there's no checking.

Immortal I heard first at round five
meant harps and wings and Nobodaddy,
drew God on some paper and crossed him out
like writing rude words in the privy.

And later Immortal was words. Then
was it I started up? Eleven,
I made my first poem about the sea,
recall I felt curiously forgiven.

Searching that out brings more up.
I never really believed in the dead
till Aunt Agnes was small wax
in the front parlour, voice ended.

Or was it the guinea-pig, the snake
with its head crushed, crimson and green,
or the kittens that left the bucket clay,
cold wet gloves with the bones still in?

Backwards is forwards in this. To look
at the learnt deaths no more than a guess
at whose ending? Not mine! Not mine!
Essentially, I escape the mess.

And escape it where? Back to thirty-five,
half-way to never, the old wheel
rutting its journey till spokes shiver
into an absolute of the real?

Or cloud-pink, hymn-sick, goody-where,
everyone loving, and God big
as a child's Christmas, outside
atheists getting over their jag?

Or maybe the bigger subtler words —
Life-Force, World-Soul, one with One:
burying one's head in this paper bag
is no way to get history done.

And something, God alone knows what,
must get done somehow. Why so?
God knows that too, if He exists,
or can know at all, being out of the show.

So we get nowhere. That's where we get.
A lemming's gallop, an ant's scuttle,
preserving the race of lemmings, ants.
Our children demand we lose the battle.

Now, however, I make truce,
today take stock, pause, reload.
I can't win, but I'll see I set
time a tough proposition, by God!

First, I have taught a few hundred
to teach some thousands the wrong things,
disrupting the state with good verse,
bad scholarship, and hard drinking.

Second, I've brought a few poets up
to distrust literature, and keep

obscenity handy for bad laws,
prigs, and academic sheep.

Third, I've defeated a sly hope
of foozling my way to Reputation
by telling the truth at least some of the time,
and always on unsuitable occasions.

Fourth, I have made poems — good, bad,
indifferent, mystical, obscene —
that someone may want when I am dead
to keep off the guilt and the bad dream.

Four. And that's all. I make no claim
for helping the tribe with fine kids.
Good or bad, I'm too much stuck
on the way they are young to make bids.

I can't say I've ever done a good deed
out of the common. I've passed by
beggars and charities and pain
with a full pocket and a dry eye.

I've kept no commandment I can recall,
having killed by proxy and by word
and broken the rest in good style,
scorning my neighbour, and cursing God.

Not much of a record. And what's ahead?
Poems till I drop, and words, words,
words. It's my trade — the black keys
clicking the tragic and the absurd.

And maybe some change. When the blood thins
I will die a little, and grow old
as gracelessly as I can to keep
some heat against the ultimate cold.

No more than that. I ask no praise,
and beg no comfort, my one prayer
I keep my heart and wit enough
to get me God alone knows where.

THE WAKING

Tonight's my birth-night. I can't sleep. One leg
twitches and jerks. It was broken at the thigh
when I was born, and now it has remembered.
The body thinks chronology aside

and 2 a.m. casts lendings off. I turn,
bullying the springs, resentfully to mutter
at that limb's dull ache, as I resent,
all too often, the stiffening of another

that remembers farther darker acts,
casting the mind out gasping. Wide awake,
I rise, walk through the house. My children sleep,
steering through dreams and accidents that come back

always to man and womanhood, trapped, staring,
on such a night as this, at shaking blind,
faint shadowed ceiling, sightless dangling bulb,
with thinking body and with helpless mind.

ALISON JANE SKELTON
Aged One

This infant staggerer carries round
in clutched fist doll and animal —
splayed ragged arms and flayed face,
chewed wet fur, torn paws. Her falls
are sudden squats on the claimed ground,
her lunges trials of guessed space.

Triumphant tyranny in her clutch
and huge cry shakes us to the heart;
the clenched assertion of her stare
and random language tugs apart
each easy sentiment; her pink
fat hands grub realistic floors.

Small pities have no place in her,
love a demand, intolerant, plain,
for food or service; tears dried,
withdrawn into her own again,
she tramples doll and animal
strewn carelessly across the wide

expanse of all the place she knows.
Can years bring alteration here,
or will she, in her private strength
of woman, keep this hidden near,
unknown of watcher, listener, friend,
or conquering lover, till, at length,

necessity and will combine
in summoning her to wake again
the pitiless tyrannic bent
of her own self-absorbment? Then,
will she be strong, who, small, is strong,
and force life to replenishment?

A SON SLEEPING
for Nicholas

So far, so good. I daren't commit myself
to anything more certain, but so far
it's pretty good, would set me up for life
if I weren't wise to how life knocks you down.
Anyway, I'm here. And he. We both. Together.
Compact in one another at this time.
He has a look of me, same dragged down mouth.
Maybe the same kink brings the same distress.
No matter. Time will tell. But time has tolled
its bells too loud for me now fingers ring
the changes of a fatherhood. He'll drive
his plough above the bones of my quick dead.

It's to be expected. We expect,
by destiny bound, each man to stand above
the cradle with his epitaph to hand,

while hands that rock the cradle learn to rule
out any copybook and only pray
Gentle upon him be your hands, my God,
always your presence; let him not believe
and doubt together; let him not attempt
the reasoned emptiness, the cleansing mind.

So far it's easy. Keep your pecker up.
Retain the casual lightness of this tone.
Joke a little. Innocent and flesh,
he sleeps his paradox while you unsolve
the ready answers, tracing each truth back
to how his first stare told you all's unknown.
And all is still unknown. It would be good
to stand aside and pay the moral out
into the labyrinth someone else explores
but, unfortunately, that can't be done,
the thread lost, rotten, frayed, too short by half,
and I half wish I'd let the whole thing drop.

But not *him*. No. I think it's clear he is,
and, being, is as much as time my way
and my existence. I can only hope
he has strong children without facing death.
May he be strong as animals are strong,
and kind and gentle, not think overmuch
of where we are. So I would disinherit
my next days from his companionship
to save him finding my way into...hell?

Hell is a big word, but I'll let it stay.
To see and find is to fear dark and loss,
and we are mortal. There's the nub, my son.
You have brought death in your two fumbling hands.
And life, of course. It makes one see how God,
(if it were God), was God in being born.
This birth brings God to me, is God perhaps,
renewing, altering, transforming death.
Now I've succeeded. Something has got out.
Words in a pattern. Thoughts upon a string.

So far, so good. I can't get farther now.
Words have walked out on me. This quiet end
of every exploration at the centre
of the labyrinth must wait for truth,
(if truth there is), must wait in presence of
a doubt and a belief and all my love
held in his fingers. Love is the last word.
To love is mortal, and death stirs at love.

CHILD

Tattered by light,
the child may see
deception in
an apple tree:

though singing birds
entrance the bough
his world is rocked
by here and now

till dark in bed
his moments come
to watch the other
side of sun,

as to his window
silent sky
swings a dreadful
finity.

The blowing wind
throughout his room
curls him smaller
in the gloom

till daylight come
to shred again
his apple tree
with leaf of pain.

THE BIRTH

What was seed, was fish,
was her hard love
engrossing his, was gilled,
was tailed, was curled
and bagged in waters,
what was blind, was deaf,
was pipelined on
the bloodthrob of the world;
what was gentle flutters
in the night,
was swelling pride,
was troubled sleep, was dry
gaped mouth, closed eyes,
tight-coiled and leaping spring,
now drags through lungs
man's terrible first cry.

UNDERGROWTH

I journey backwards.
Ahead is nothingness.
At forty-one
there's little in the mind
but thoughts of origins,
a primal speck,
the clutching branches
of a falling tree.

I hack my way through undergrowth.
Some girls
prefer an older man :
their loves are tight,
their nipples urgent;
out on Clover Point
the split moon spills
its monies in the sea

and through my slippery fingers.
I can't hold
the minute any more;
each windscreen swipe
rubs out the possible:
I see her home,
become her father
gnashing in his grave.

What was is where you are.
Who could take on
that cluttered fury?
Dreams and limitations
choke the tangling light.
I see my first
girl staring from
a stiff-necked photograph

with pigeons at her back.
Upon his column
rigid Nelson
wets his one blind eye
nostalgically.
Yellow dusk descends.
I choke upon a
twenty-year-old fog

and stagger farther.
Here I am alone.
The ruined summer-house
remembers crimes
against the spiders;
wasps blaze in a jar
hung from the warped
suggestion of a twig,

and summer is all springtime.
Flickering here,
the images move fast;
the little deaths
reduplicate and blur;
the books become
a single story

playing out the gods'
heroic roles and masteries,
conquering nettles
taller than my thigh.
I stumble, drop
upon the warm crisp grass;
within me echoes
mesh and alter;
everything's at odds

still in this garden world,
though, dreaming forwards,
energy becomes itself
and time
a countless multitude.
Crowds hurry past
on backward journeys,
faces dark, confused,

ridiculous. The tree's
about to fall.
The undergrowth is filled
with scurrying cries.

THE SPARROWS

From a sour garden wrinkled with trees
in the well of yellow houses, tall
as yesterday's syllables, the birds,
plucking at crumbs, step into mind,
random and delicate, with all
the desperate aplomb of their kind.

Looking for language fit to start
the paved flanks of this place between
yesterday's shibboleths and let
the needling logos split the hard
imprisoning stone, is to say green,
say music, is to live aloud

until the deafened paving break.
From that sour garden webbed with trees
twelve sparrows step into my mind,
random and delicate. Around
the desperate ease of time's mistake
the pick pick of these birds resounds.

TENACITY

Achievement?
It is enough to be alone,

certainty
unrecognized by applause

but long familiar,
bark growing

season by season
over the gripping hand.

FORTY

At forty sensual enough, no grey
at jaw or temple, though beneath each eye
the softly folded skin announces years
of peering in the brown and emptying glass,
I recognize myself, could sketch the mouth's
disconsolate swerve, the nose, the tilted head.

This is achievement of a kind. When young,
I could amaze myself with my own stare
and touched discovery each time I reached
the razor to my cheek. Now nothing's new
but comprehension. Each road I have walked
rewards each footfall with a vacant gaze.

I rack my long-imprisoned brain. Complete
and stuck with that accomplishmenent, I probe
philosophies to swear I'll be reborn,
pay tailors to transform the usual, break
habits, friendships, promises, contrive
a fresh evasion for each humdrum doubt.

Yet I remain myself. A woman's bed,
that changing-room of truth, can dress me up
in clownish finery only for the night
or the tempestuous moment. Mornings shake
each lending loose, and I can never find
a different mastery on the downward stair,

but only this Familiar, blandly gross
with confidence, firm-set in his old ways,
foul-breathed, libidinous, who at the end
when I lie sick will mutter thrrough the room
his worn discordances, his usual prayers,
and mumble in my pillow friendly lies.

A PIECE OF ORANGE PEEL

Coloured the incredible flame
of the blaze in a child's picture book,
skin pocked and pitted like the moon's,
it curls on the pavement, a pothook
of some giant scribbler whose word stopped
short of its comment and went slack.

The blinds are drawn. At the very end
fingers like sucked bones touched the Book
as touching wood; her shrill breath
reached for a word, but fell back;
her eyes gaped and then closed
on a blaze of pain that turned black

The pith, scuffed, ragged, a torn swerve
of dirty yellow, spongy, sore,
has not yet dried ; a film of dust

and specks of soot adhere where four
self-congratulating flies
settle and ticklishly explore.

All over, they closed her eyes
that had flicked open again to stare
on her first true blindness. Hands
washed, dried, dressed, combed the grey hair
that crackled and sputtered, the black Book
moved on to the bedside chair.

Kicked and downtrodden, the peel snaps;
blackened, crisped, and dried thin
as a lathe-shaving, it awaits
rainflood or broomstroke to begin,
and in another street the hands
that made it tear at skin again.

THE TRACK TO THE SEA

Here is the track, between rocks,
down to the shore; torn rags
of brown weed caress the headland
with lift and sag of a dead hand.
This is the edge of everything.
My stick impales a clench of burrowing
waste-paper, and rat-tats the rust
of nameless cylinders. Our years are cast
upon abandonment, the suck and drag
of transformation. Half in sand, a dog,
becoming architechture, washes clean
the stench of appetite with fugual bone.

I walk here Sundays, knowing that I live,
decaying and abrupt to shock of wave,
until my eyes are pools, my fingers curl
about the chalk-stiff spirals of a shell,
a mere absurdity. Some yards offshore
a boat rocks like a wish, sways to the steer
of endless counterpoint, and, turning back,

all harmonies grown strange, I have to shake
my head to hear a word, throw out the sand
before the house can settle. We exist
only because the sea is patient and
refuses us until we cannot rest
in anything but echoes of the mind.

ON THE EVE OF ALL HALLOWS

Histories walk tonight ;
clad in accomplished fate,
each takes his grievous turn ;
candles in turnips burn
their spearblades on the dark
and quiver in the talk,
the after-silence. Here,
at the old end of the year,
I was born. My star
rose in this watchful mirror.

Now quiet is possessed
by necessary ghosts;
they too, born in between
the tide and the tugging moon,
found violence in the nerve,
had pity, suffered love,
and ached at beauty. Death
sighs on our common breath
and mirror. Ghosts, stand by
this poet of your family.

Poetry has been my line
from snivelling childhood on;
I have the usual scars,
the usual haunted face,
am lecherous enough;
I even have a cough,
though so far don't spit blood;
I plague my wife: it's said
Art is the one thing for
which everyone must suffer.

I stare down at the glass;
behind me my own face
encounters me; I turn
and parings twist my name;
my own words fill my ears.
What will survive ? The stars
may tell in time, at least
will sieve away the worst,
and probe with practised hand
the desolate remainder.

It is one thing to build
a poem and fix the world
around it, make it spin,
another to give stone
the lasting, bitten word.
Ghosts, listen. You have had
mortality's one proof;
I ask you for relief:
tell me these passions are
in more than the mind's mirror.

Some say poems have kept
a thought from being trapped
by staying on the move
like most wise beasts we have,
and some think them a mode
of clambering inside
the space between the fear
and the resultant prayer
of every man that wants
to last out the long moment.

I'd say mine were the lies
I had to fix in place
to keep Truth on the run,
for when the hunt is done,
the quarry faced, who knows,
as blood streams in the eyes,
what fingers grip? My hands
for purely mortal ends
tie knots which they untie
with difficulty, intently.

Nothing in me is fixed,
and nothing I have asked
comes from a firm desire;
I have no final prayer
tonight as my words all
turn ghosts within the still
and reckoning hour I face;
I claim no special grace,
for all my deaths are on
the point of being human.

I keep the mirror clean;
I watch it change, alone
with love of every nerve
of living that we have,
and see time unpick time.
I do not wear a name
except the end of speech.
The stars rock. And I reach
up from the drowning glass
my small necessities.

THE FORTIETH SUMMER

At forty we are restless. I peel dry skin
gingerly from my back, a paper-thin
opaque elastic covering; a snake
does it in one; I do it patch by patch,
and wince as hairs are tugged. One touch of sun
on forty years of sun and protection tears,
revelatory. On the dunes a girl
plays Nausicaa to Ulysses, that old
wry sailor telling lies to risk belief
one summer day at least. I squat on sand.
Truth troubles me, all easy ignorance gone.
Yet, patch by patch, the vulnerable insists
upon existence, hair by pulling hair
disclosing rawness. Better rub in oil;
better avoid the glare. Could be my daughter
lying there, her wagging cigarette

childhood insouciance, her make-up some
important temporary high-school craze
without direction. Smile. Call over. Say
nonsense, rubbing off the dying skin
to make sensation itch. At forty, one
finds summer grown so short there's but a day
to burn away the dead. Her mouth is red.
Troy smoulders in the past, ash-grey, ash-grey.

TIGER, TIGER

Sleep's grown a killer;
jungle fills my eyes;
sweat is a skin for the night,
a viscous clad.
Turn me over, boot;
there is blood from my ear:
slack and heavy, I
lie heavy and slack.

My daughter, leaden-eyed
in her night-dress, wanders
down the stairs from her nightmare.
It is still
four o'clock in the morning.
The house is a box.
Voices rattle like dice.
Is our number up?

I once could challenge her night,
but my snarl is dry.
Someone has measured my length
and examined my skin.
The gun butt at my nape
is a wooden god.
I pull myself upstairs
like a sack of rags,

mouthing what dead things mouth:
Be easy, happy!

Uncle is very well.
We are all very well.
Mother sends you her love.
Be happy, easy!
I think I am losing contact...
She falls asleep.

And back below the trees
it is hotter, darker.
If I could stretch one claw
I could scratch a stone's
pelt of wet moss,
tatter the mark of my name
so that a month would pass
before it was gone,

but my claw can't stretch.
It is nearly time
for the knife to open me up,
for the skin to be slit
away from the weight of muscle.
The baby cries,
a kite in the high, mad sky.
More kites. More cries.

And the earth beneath me heaves.
My wife is rising.
When the kite's cries end
and the baby is fed,
I am plundered to deafness,
only the slide
and clatter of beaks,
the random noises of feeding

nibbling at total darkness.
Here is here
the solid and the abyss,
the real and the dread.
What was the cause of my name?
Has the blood remembrance?
Heavy and slack, I lie
with glass for eyes.

THE NINTH MONTH

Ninth month ending,
nights are long. The house
echoes earlier children ;
footsteps, slamming doors
drive the stillness crazy.
Stillness is still
with waiting; eyes are dark;
fullness touches all.

Bags packed, cupboards crammed
with diapers and talc,
shopping lists like lists
for the long-travelling dead
upon their painted ships,
what is it I forget?
Phone numbers of the near.
Cards for the distant shores.

The simple taut event:
she must become a beast
whose single primal urge
possesses every squirm.
The fingers of the leaves
tug at the aching sun;
the river fills the cavern;
cloudbanks spill the moon.

We fuss and potter, count
the minutes between pangs,
and swear at slowness, share
our mockeries and absurd
resentments, try a book,
switch on T.V., pretend
we are not making spells,
do not revere the dark,

the all-engrossing god,
the breasted one, the gross-
bellied patience, wise
in store of life and loss.

Yet nights are long; we kneel
by secret in our nights :
the god is generous, waits,
miraculous, endures.

THE BEGINNING

First Light: the mouth
begins to taste itself and lick
misshapen breath alive;
the eyes are wet with fur;
slowly claws recede
and forests dwindle; scent
abandons cunning; hands
are hands at human sheets.

Gradual muscles harden.
Redness hits the sun.
Down in the sudden bushes
owl and badger sleep
their intricate small dawn
as summer bares its flanks.
The earth is baked to crack.
Trout rot in the stream.

These swollen-bellied days
the sky is empty, drained
of passion and intent;
the flies are idle words
half-heard and half-dismissed;
you move out from our bed,
distended belly taut,
and wade across the room.

You move into the day,
a woman shouldering sea,
your eyes the brown collapse
of seaweed upon rock,
your buttocks ruined hills,
your limbs colossus; now

creation is its tide
and you will have it turn.

You stand at open door
and call the waters down.
The leaves turn in the wind.
The grass begins to shake.
The sea lies very still.
You spit upon a stone
and make the spiders run.
Air tightens in my throat.

The waters gather, gather.
Behind my face the beast
sleeps aftermaths of dark
that you may hear the dream
and make the tidal turn.
You eat the meat I give.
Air trembles to embrace
the final, human cry.

THE ANNIVERSARY
to Sylvia

Something is changing.
I have sloughed off a skin.
Maybe time is leaving time behind
trapped in the familiar
clothes and clocks
that muffle every touch of hand on hand;
maybe, simply,
I become the change
of life to life,
and, eager to unbind,
confuse the ropes I
tremble to have off:
your head discomforts me;
I ache with love.

Ten years, almost.
Why should the years change
familiarity to passion, press
my sudden happiness
upon a flesh
grown heavy with child-bearing
and remote?
Why should I long for you?

I see a girl
sharp-boned with purities
turn to my arms
and touch the little
pulsings of her throat
to lie back under trees.
Cars ravage by.
Our eyes meet across tables
and we die
absurd small deaths of
secrecy and ease.

Ten years of you.
I am newborn to this
habitual living
troubled by a kiss,
the usual spent,
this new unusual come.
Put out your hand.
I have sloughed off a skin.
Familiars all are gone to earth.
A green
decade begins again.
And we begin.

Travelling Time

TIDYING THE STUDY

Steering the weeks towards that sudden
break with earth, the widening patch of light
under the steel dark, between blade and stone,
my hands turn over papers. This is how
I curled my fingers to force out Her name,
defying emptiness, and this how She
reponded. Letters. Photographs. A word
that stuck out like a nail. A picture hangs
uneasily. I time its taking down
as one more moment of departure, gaining
back the past arrivals and departures
as if gathering up the all that was
into this nearing journey. We respond
equally to necessity and dream,
unsure which is the dream and which the need.
Should I put down this feather on this shelf
how long will it remain? And will it change
into a symbol separate from my touch,
or, clutched by tenants' children, snap and fall
to the loud vacuum of a tidying mind?
I put it there. The softness bares its teeth.
The blackness quivers. I see Icarus
suddenly loving the familiar maze
and suddenly ashamed. This book must go.
I never read it, never will. It thumps
upon the stack of Vogues, the worn-out clothes.
Out there, somewhere, extends the lip of land
from which I'll move upon a breath exhaled
in roars of foghorn , feathers of the smoke
shaking and lucent. There was time for life
once in this huddling room. Now, nearly done,
I push the last book in the final carton,
stand up, ease my back. There's nothing sure
but that departure lets us learn the shore.

THE CAVES OF DRACH (MALLORCA)

Every travelling is of the soul
seeking its station. Through the Caves of Drach
above the Middle Sea clear water brims
the mirror imagery of hanging swords
and stalagmitic heroes that, half-born,
part man, part muscling clay, transfixed as stone,
hint epics of the upper world. The flanks
we brush are glistenings of polished bone
and wet and chill to fingers as we crowd
faceless and nameless down through narrowing halls
to where the water waits to hear us sigh
our turquoise wonder, our reflected awe
at Memory's glass. We have been here before
on this descent from light into the cave
above the sea, the dangerous ante-room
of tide and time and mortal burdening limbs.
My younger daughter writhes, jumps, points, begins
to pull away. I hold her fast. It seems
odd to prevent her passion for her dreams
in caves my love has made her travel through,
for Time's a phantom, Death a glancing blow
forgotten on the farther hurrying track.
My son says Dragon is our word for Drach. . . .
Caves of the Dragon. . . . I assent. We face
mythic probabilities in this place
and fear our certainties, for every step
shows life and passion poised before their leap
into the gross and mortal ; every gasp
is tribute to our loss. I watch my sleep
extending everywhere its carven walls;
my dreams reach to my dreams, touch, and are fused;
my tears are pillars in an ageless night.
Only the Guide's contrivance of a light
enables me to think of my own name,
own hands, own wife, own children. Should it dim
or dwindle into black I would become
simply the changing music that has run
through here since spirit let our time begin,
and would be nothing, everything, and all
eternity of pause, for here we stay
before birth's thrust, and here we slowly turn

percipience into need and need to form,
each one of us. But now the tide moves on,
mumbling and jostling. Boats await. The man
beside the oar, a shifting shape of black,
drives us towards our landing. Memory wakes
blurred voice, blind vision, and the daylit dark.

ROCAMADOUR
for John Montague

A sword thrust into stone
as if it had split the cliff
open with one lunge :
the long crack extends,
dry-lipped, white,
an open astonished scar,
down from the rust red blade
above the holy dark
where the black Virgin holds
impassively the straight-
backed saviour of the world
as if the world were real
to Her and Her alone.

I look up at the sword.
Words of the old Romance
alter before the fact.
There was a human hand,
a human head (now skull),
and sweat and slippery blood,
even a bursting lung
that sent the death-cry out
across the startled miles
and drew an army down.

There was a man. A nail
from the True Cross can pierce
acceptance with belief :
there's no doubt in the hand
that holds, can hold, has held,

for love demands a sign
and not a proof; the sword
stands barefaced out from rock,
improbable and sure
as the black Virgin throned
and crowned within the dim
devotional light.
           I stand
where image and image meet,
relic to relic brought.
The earth dissolves. The sword
and Virgin rest secure
in more than crown and stone;
they have accomplished what
no History dare pretend :
they have extended Truth
beyond the grasp of fact.
Here I must stand and claim
my right to have my death
and think my vision real,

for what is real is real
in vision, not in fact:
the eye contains the world
and not the world the eye.
The sword is Roland's sword;
it cleaved the timeless rock.
The Virgin healed the King.
All virtue still endures
upon this love-worn stone
and heals me of my hurt.
I bear an ivory horn
that only when I die
can touch its final chord
and sound the vision pure
and plunge my soul to rest
beside Her in the rock.

ROBERT GRAVES IN DEYA, MALLORCA

A single rock,
the pierced ear of the sea,
below the Deya road,
and by the road
the village guardian,
a lone stone pine
overlooking hills
of terraced rock,
establish ambience.
In any place
a hundred poems have spoken
there is this
assertion by the landscape:
it may be
in crag, or lake, or cave,
or broken tower
fanged against sunset
or a flight of swans
blessing the still lake water
under trees,
but always in that place
earth frees its themes.
There dreams evolve through earth
and earth through dreams
till every image
is of both and one
with every happening
of speech and stone.

So Deya is, because of him.
He comes
down to the terrace,
underneath his arm
a basket of black olives,
on his head
the straw hat of a peasant
from the fields,
a strong, worn, honoured man
admiring earth.

Lemons and oranges
flare within the green
below the terrace edge
and sapling beech
(boca and book)
are offerings at his door.

Poetry is studying
how the spirit soars
on learned as on simple
ignorant things.
An inch-long Pegasus,
its green-bronze wings
arrogant, fragile,
stands upon a sill.
The stone house throbs and
echoes like a bell.

Events are of belief
and not of act.
All history is credence,
and all truth
the image of an ambience
that exacts
the proper tribute
from the humbled mind.
So Poetry knows,
knows more the less it proves.
Explain? said Goethe,
*I will not explain
anything I have written.*
Vision lives
that one dimension
closer to the sun
than all we measure by,
and Time, absurd,
becomes a mesh of shadows
cast by that
entrancing light poets enter
to meet Death
in every poem they make
and be reborn
by virtue of the poem

which alters earth
around them.
        Thus in Deya,
as we talk,
the sapling beeches
reach up to the sun
the natural language
of the timeless Muse
who is the Light that casts
these shadows, words.

Conclusions are not.
Everything attends
the every scene and minute.
Though we part,
a hand stays on a book,
a basket set
upon a wall holds olives
black with light
and oranges burn, picked,
upon the trees
that are both seed and kindling,
fruit and flame.
What matters is not scholarship
or fame
but being both of shadow
and of light,
of root and air,
of furnace and of sea,
of Time and of
eliminated Time.

We drive from Deya,
bearing Deya home.

THREE POEMS FOR TWO TRAVELLERS

I

I have not been where you are going.
You have not been, and no-one has ever been.
When first you recognize the fountains playing
out of a musical on the cinema screen,
do not forget your fiction. Still pretend
to be yourselves. Buy picture-postcards. And,
when back in your hotel or pension, mean
less than your signatures, or it will end.

Contemplate always your faces in the glass.
This may be pleasant, that one virile, crude.
It isn't easy to let habits pass,
but you must know the other face imbued
with more of you than yours. That mask was made
by your own fingers; this was simply laid
upon you by another, having viewed
all other possibles, and both may fade.

Keep truth at distance; truth is, after all,
that which accommodates accepted facts.
Here every fact is new. To lie at all
is an impossibility. Exact
from time a trust in fiction, and contrive
scene, action, detail, carefully. Believe
only the shared deception in each act,
and make a stillness in which both can grieve.

II

East of the station is a tall decayed
yellow and white of scribbled wall, so patched
with greys of damp and greens of crawling age,
you'd think it dying of its history. Watch
it carefully. It may be true. It may
expose the answer that you did not catch.

It is a country, certainly. The browns
and greens make landscapes troubled with the cracks

and seams of rivers. Surely here a town
squats by a mountain, and that stain, exact
and sure as any charted paper, shows
the valley that you sought for, then turned back.

Moreover, it keeps changing. Here and there
a flake of stucco falls, a mountain dies;
birds pick-axe lichens, ruining a sea
or sacred village with shrill empty cries.
There is no date upon the stone, no name.
Of such are every wanderer's obsequies.

Nevertheless, fare forward. You will go
with this map in your mind, and find it tell
as much as any about wind and snow,
climax and cataract. If all goes well
it will create for you the deepest lake
in which to plumb your heaven, or your hell.

III

I hear a story of an old blind man
lives in a huge pile across the bay,
read to morning afternoon evening
by two that have lost their way.
This you will see. The great paintings
burn on the walls; old gods
gesture and copulate, old eyes
watching from faun and satyr heads.

This you will visit. And one will say,
offering you goblets, 'Drink'. Drink
nothing, nor eat. These are chained
to the heart's darkness. Do not think
it an old tale, your fear born
of the wrong century, and grow kind.
Can you be sure in this country
the gods are dead, or the man blind?

Who was it swore his nerves strong,
retina lucid, mind clear,
limbs supple? If he moves

he moves crabwise in a wheel chair,
hunched, head down ; if he speaks, speaks
melodiously. Do not take
his hand or his wine. There is no time
to take that pathway through heartbreak.

AT TUTANKHAMUN'S TOMB, THINKING OF YEATS

I enter the tomb and remember
his chanted, laden words.
On fresco and papyrus gods
have the hooked heads of birds.
The flared dark echoes. The still golden
smile haunts and disturbs.

Artifice of a dead thing
mocks the hands that made,
the bestial tunnelling
into the mountain side,
and the inscribing eye
mastering laquer and jade.

Broken complexities
of the meshed nerve and vein
build coloured hieroglyphs
on wood and stone.
Past mire and fury phrase
peace on long bed and crown.

All that man is in his time
of laboured passion and need
is to accompany the journey
of the painted dead
whose toys and kingdoms rest,
is to guard the smiling head

skinned with gold. I remember
his senatorial voice
echoing the maker's need

of a ghost's objective grace.
He built a golden bird
out of his raggedness,

and heard its clock-work sing
to emperor and queen
on Hades' bough of past
and passing and to come.
He had his thought worked out
and imaged on his tomb.

The single eye of Ra
looks cold upon his grave.
Horseman and hawk, the sun
swings by the bones that strove
huddled in dirt, or huddled
in their painted clothes.

Yet the long Pharoah looks
with epicurean eyes,
firm in surfeit, content,
with life's epiphanies
gathered at head and foot
under the stones mock skies,

and I am kneeling down
in centuries and dirt
before a bandaged death,
the withered lung and heart
praising still, the small skull
still catafalqued in art.

Such sinews thonged and dried
rig every argonaut,
hang every fanatic oath,
and rock all bells' tongued weight;
umbilicus and cord
rope sands to keep us caught,

and that gilt smile the dark
conceals as torches burn
out in lifted hands
retains its living form,

and, passionate and gay,
it's stillness will return

through time to what we made
when centuries beaten flat
above our journeying dead
are broken into dirt,
and years fall down like stones
before the reaching heart,

and, chronicled with lives
burned out to give us bread,
bound by the nerve and vein,
we lie untenanted
below the desert's waste
and know that we are dead.

For then that smile shines out,
as gods with heads of birds
and stick-legged scribes pretend
dead empery disturbs,
ghosts journey on in state.
His laden wrought-out words

leave as I leave the tomb,
this history ill begun
that must end in the dark
and passionate painted room
some-one disturbs, disturbed, behind
his back the bird-beaked sun.

THE FAREWELL

I talk of *Amours de Voyage.* You shake your head,
admitting ignorance. I feel the bruise
spread through your fingers that accept the book.
Your body, stiffened by those Northern snows,
cannot believe in Mediterranean ease
and antiquarian elegance. Your eyes
expect the green of ice, the iron trees

black-spurred against the roar of cutting wind.
Voices come down from there. The joy of dogs.
The broken windows. All the rubbled creeds
in hugger-mugger, whisky-drunk. You shake
your head again, hair like a copper wave
burnished and burning. There is little use
in talk of elegance, of poised control,
where icepacks loom. You cannot find a track
that does not lead you through the blinded snows
to solitude, the blow upon the face,
the rending animals, the boot and claw.
You smile as children smile when tears are done,
less to reward than comfort those who must
not learn the heart's a stone. Your hand is cold.
No-one can ever dispossess their world
for any other. Neither Clough nor I.
My farewell spreads its stain across your sky
but does not change it. Conversation veers.
We'll meet again perhaps. A couple of years.
Three at the most. When I return. Who knows?
I watch you walk away into the snows.

THE VIRGIN OF TORCELLO

For James Fitzsimmons

An alley of old statues
under tangled vines,
olives, figs — Roman,
Venetian, Florentine, Greek
of six hundred years
standing among the vines,
a gross of old statues :
the sky is blue, sun hot.

Images phrase our selves
blanched by an ideal sun
in postures that reward
perspectives of the blind
search for flesh as god.
We move into the cold

echoings of a church
from which an empire fell

and find Her carven wood,
the young mouth unkissed,
the heavy robes alert
only to sudden winds
across the earthen floor
of pity's simple house,
the shading cowl a sleep
of twilight on the mind.

And yet the soft eyes lift
up under almond lids
in ecstasy or pain;
only the eyes have moved
away from girlhood; stilled
by vision, rapt, the long-
boned hands are small, at rest

as we are not at rest
between the clustering vines,
or where the pomegranates
burn within a green
more vivid than a cry
against the soft-flushed stone
of Her own campanile
with its bronze-green bell.

She is our peace, our past.
We have walked shallow steps
of baptism through clear water.
The pool is murkier now,
the long stones slippery, and
one door is blocked by chunks
of marble. Yet for Her
I find I almost kneel

as lion, ox, or lamb
might kneel to lap the chill
clarities of a love
that lifts these half-lost stones
alive into the light

of wisdom, not of sun.
The statues flake, decay;
moss gathers to their groins

and on one roof a boy,
part writhing creeper, wears
a conscious smile of ease;
a woman bears an urn
above ripe naked breasts;
an old man's beard grins;
the pomegranates blaze;
and there is no return

to that which gave Her form
its girlhood and its trust
in words from out the dark.
The water silts with mud.
Our boat must bear us west
upon the stale canal
between the withering vines
of our disquietude.

LINES UPON VIEWING THE GILDED EQUESTRIAN STATUE OF KING WILLIAM THE THIRD AT KINGSTON-UPON-HULL

You have a good seat, bright-saddled
along the canyon of grey stone
that ends at the river. You look strong,
seem undeniably at home
in the dazzle of self-reflected light;
nothing has altered,nothing gone.

A cat can look at a King, a poet
apostrophise Royalty; here goes: —
Under that armour your bones are wind,
your heart a hollow, and who knows
what great advantage that can give
a king poised in trampling shadows?

Assurance, of course, the first. A dumb
and blinding ignorance can outweigh
almost all fact. To you the smoke
from the smeared ships dips in curtsey,
the stagger and slap of drunk boots
echo salutes of a guards, volley.

Or am I wrong, King Billy, King
of the hollow legs and the gilt grin?
Is it maybe that the dead night
whistles up wit in your bones of wind
and your hands uncramp and your eyes turn,
finding a different reign begin?

I know some say it's a trick of the light
makes the late walker jump back
from a hoof that moves, but I know, too,
drunks have been found with their skulls cracked
and girls have screamed. One dawn
a pile of horse droppings steamed black.

Students, of course! And a good joke!
You're dead as a bright brass doorknob torn
from a long dead door and sold in the market
to God-knows-who from the junk stall.
Dead. Dead. Dead....I start again
with a child of death in a gold caul.

No. Not that. It was somewhere else
that sentence happened, not in this street
where the pigeons litter your head with white
and newspaper blows between your feet
and lorries pass and the river there
at the end of the road is grey with sweat.

You're dead, but not Death, King Billy. Done.
Finished. Hollow. A glittering shell.
And yet that image returns to haunt,
drifting up with the river smell,
sickening, confusing; the far shore
seems greener than anyone could tell.

But this is ridiculous. Civic pride
is the only cause of that hollow core
where the winds may whistle or may not....
And as for the light on that far shore —
Purely coincidence. Today
it happens there's sunlight. Nothing more.

But I must admit I am troubled still.
Something somewhere contains the Truth,
and why not you? One hoof is lifted —
but is it always the same hoof?
No gold King trampled Sodom down,
the sceptic swears, but where's his proof?

ENTERING FIRENZE

Faces invent the past.
A priest in black,
head by Bellini,
sits in a corner seat,
vein-ribbed hands at rest,
mouth down-drawn, cheeks
ascetic, channelled.
Outside, hills maintain
the furious thwarts
and chasms of a green
blackened beyond each martyrdom.
Sebastian
enters at Milano
still unstained.

And what there is in Art
that baffles, baffles;
eternity perplexes us
with eyes
that hold the light
of visionary encounters
caught by the plaster
under sounding bells
and change the world to memory.
Entering Firenze,

Here Shelley wrote...
Here Petrarch, Dante...
                              Round
stones are skulls
beneath my feet. I reach
my hands through air, plague-struck.
No words. No words.
The heads that mass the street
are every one
authority and age.
By the Uffizzi
a sea-god
in a wilderness of birds
writhes dumbly under centuries.
I bear
History like a wretched
beggar back
to those that made it,
crying out for alms.

CALANCHE DE PIANA (CORSICA)

for Molly Hargreaves

Runnelled and fanged,
the red rock
squints across fissures,
hangs masks
of prayer and laughter,
hard red tears
writhing, altering,
till my hand
holding her hand
twists, stiffens,
gnarls, the last
grasp of a tree
knotted with olives
in a land
of sour spittle
and harsh words.

Pausing upon this
track to seek
out the particular
racked angel,
the raw appropriate
emblem, trapped
emulant of
the heart's inferno,
I discover
nothing less
than the topography
of lost
Paradise,
its channelling tears,
brilliant as acid,
burning bowls
from which rain spills
down riven limbs
to wash out walls,
roads, tombs, and sluice
the miriad slim knives
of the great
gum trees, hold
in globes of light
the spiked green orbs
of chestnuts, rage
through breaking campaniles
and find,
watching my claw hand
hold tight
to bone and muscle,
every sag
and wrinkle
of unheroic flesh
also eroding,
altering, burning,
fathering its masks
upon the world.

BURNING STICKS, MALLORCA

for Anthony Kerrigan

Poems should be wisdom
or be love.
      I burn
dry sticks to incense
that this orchard hill
may blossom rich, fruit heavy,
fill the Spring
with radiance, and the belly
with good meat.
It is enough to labour
if with trust
in wholeness of the earth
and gods, (or God),
setting the furrow
or remaking words,
carving the ancient olive wood,
or, hunched
above clay, giving spirit
simple forms—
king, soldier, angel, bull.
Each man must turn
what is into what is
or he will die
as buildings die
left tenantless and soiled
beside forgotten fields.
Beyond this bay
sea stretches to the first
names of our world,
the broken images
of moon and sun,
hoarded and crumbling,
and yet what was done
remains a frame for learning
and for thought.
The fence-posts round this olive grove
are wrought
as phalluses;
this white clay figurine,

(crowned, virile, potent,
fresh as earliest dawn),
is one of those
that only virgins may
create to plead fruition,
and the play
of bull and man still wounds
the timeless sky.
Tine is the earth's
most ample perfidy.

Poems should be timeless
and of time.
      We change
little but names
and accidents.
      We fall
upon one earth
and with one mouth applaud
one harvest
and cry one cry of despair.

Poems should be timeless
and be love.
      They prove
little but movements
of the hearts they move,
concerned to celebrate
not spell the truth.
The love that puts
this message in my mouth
may be my own
but is not mine alone.
The smoke of incense
rises from the stone
by my intent
but not by my own will;
it is the will of being's self
that fills
the crowding blossom
with the gentle haze
and asks the mountains
for their certainties.

BERNARDINO LUINI (LUGANO)

To hold on stone, exactly,
the nature of story,
its hurl and lift,
its caverns,
its hills and weirs,
and the inescapable
human pathos,
the green and blue of cloth
caught upon thighs,
and the lifted arm
laying bare the pulse
of agony at the throat
and the soldiers fighting
is not enough
There must be other dimensions,
the catch in the speaker's voice,
his gaze in tears,
and the smell of the wreckage of centuries
burning, burning
till suffocation bursts
in a gasp of light
and all the impossible children.
There must be
everything in one instant,
before and after
simply variations upon one scene
which is that of discovery,
time found timeless,

but, above all,
there must be
at dawn, a door
that opens full upon it,
streaming sunlight
from lake, from sky, from mountain,
so that the man
or woman, there in the door,
a shadow pointing
onwards to the vision,
stands, tormented

in an ecstasy, breathless,
gasping *My God!*
Oh, my God!, profanely
wrenched to submission.

CAMPO DEI FIORI
for Patrick Grant

The market shudders canvas;
colours gash
the light with ripeness,
yellow, green, red. Peppers,
melons, apples, pomegranates
flicker,
pile and tumble,
as five thousand fish,
heads of a congregation,
upturned all,
sing voiceless psalmodies
beside the flat
slab of ray,
a cope of blanched white flesh
spread in a field of flowers
where flame bit
the cowled philosopher
between flayed walls
and shaking stinking shadows.
At day's end
boys caper round their bonfires
as fruit roll
rotten among litter
choking fountains,
silting alleys.
Head bowed, Bruno stands
grave-browed in effigy,
forgotten reasons
imprisoning him in stillness,
leaden skirts
hanging stiff and stained
as children dance.

THE TRAVELLER

Travelling East
among scattered stones,
each day I pass
the place where I was born

and each night sleep on earth
to rise at day
and pass the same place
in the same old way,

muttering, baffled,
"Perhaps now it's done?"
But every time I sleep
the road moves on

and faster still until,
these nights, I sleep
only a little while,
for I must keep

the pace or fall behind
where crossroads trap
and helpful strangers
with defective maps.

Waking & Dreaming

THE JOURNAL

Seventeenth of November, Nineteen Sixty:
    Today looked back on friends. Today
    made a picture of a walled city
    that is also a village and a sea,
    not painted, but composed of snips of paper,
    fragments of photographs, old magazines,
    litter of travelling thirty-five years,
    (to make it a symbol, give it a good name),

    and looked back on friends. Today began
    a different contemplation. The poem starts
    somewhere within this alteration
    of the assembled documents of the heart.

Fifth of October, Nineteen Sixty Seven :
    Today looked back on words. The distance ends
    in a different place, although the difference
    seems to make no odds. Today hands,
    busy still with pictures, made a face,
    though not a face exactly but a head
    without a face — you could say anaconic
    (to give it a reference, give it a clever word),

    and looked back on words. Today began
    lack of identity, a paper world
    blowing like paper, settling into a poem
    no-one intended, and that will never be heard.

Tomorrow, or after almost a year of tomorrows,
    the statements may all be the same or all have stopped,
    the faceless head in the ambiguous place
    still altering time as it adjusts the scraps
    of hope and history, or gone from time.
    Tomorrow the sentence will still be at the start,
    searching for punctuation, gathering up
    frayed threads of meaning (to accept the part
    now of interpreter, and to begin
    a different contemplation). Journal's end
    approaches slowly. Yesterday looked back.
    Looked back today. Time tires the moving hand.

THREE PANELS FOR A QUIET HOUSE

I

Here the dawn is slow.
Half a world away
dawn is a sudden light.
My fingers trace those treees
out on your sleeping back.
You roll across your dream
and find my body hard.
The children wake below.

II

Shut me up with a wish.
It grows as big as my head
inside my head until
I let it out; it grows
into a bear as big
as the cupboard where I am,
and eats me up in a gulp.
I will not tell my wish.

III

Cold metal tastes of breath
and cold water staled
by standing long in the air;
knife, do not touch my mouth.

A knife can cut like grass,
can bend like a willow twig,
can jump up like a fish;
knife, keep from my hand.

THE VOICES

I. VOICE ON A BIRTHDAY

"Call me ancient.
I have years for teeth
and gnaw the mountains.
Every road's my spoor
and every town my droppings.
Keep me tracked.
I go to earth before a
stable door.

I have no strategy
but shame. This earth
cannot protect me
or disguise my smell,
even distracts me
with those kills whose bones
are trampled in the mud
about the stall.

Yet here for seconds
once I knelt, close-curled,
unraked by hungers,
and here wish to die
if man can dig me out
or find a way
to dowse the cruel
planet in the sky."

2. VOICE OF A WITNESS

"I am what you suppose.
Your truthful eye
hunches me over a cradle,
rewards my trend
with pathways up the hillside,
bleeds my mouth,
shakes the ridiculous
bladder in my hand.

You are never wrong.
Remember this
when I come crawling up the
final stair,
my rags untouchable,
or when I stand
like armour at the deathcell's
opening door.

I am the thing you see,
no other thing.
Do not mistrust the vision
you inform,
or for one second
listen to my voice
as if it were not vibrant
in your own."

3. VOICE FROM A CONFESSIONAL

"I am destruction
built as a machine.
Whatever engines are,
they tear their springs
and shudder into climax
of dropped steel
sheared through the holding
bolts that lock their frames.

Unction I ask
that dribbles loose as weed
down burnished axles,
triggering their shafts'
enormous wandering,
isolated in
strength unrelated to
my proper task.

I have no product but
my self that wears
out rhythms of its
dislocating drive
to end stock-still, belts broken,

looking out
upon the land
it hungered to believe."

4. VOICE OF A FINALIST

"At last I have self-destruction.
I have removed,
piece by piece, each part of
my whole body,
have finally, in an act of
ultimate logic,
emptied my bag of seed on the
road in spit.
Nothing whole remains.
I walk my shadow
carefully round corners
in case the sun,
trapped by a church or
tenement, refuses
even the semblance that
with twisting hands
plays animals upon the
walls or knits
endlessly cats cradles
for lost children."

5. INSTRUCTIONS

"Trust me.
I am the god,
the hassock beneath the tree,
the pyx in the rock-pool.
                              Never
is one word I will say.

Kiss me.
I am the bride,
the heat in the seashore lace,
the breast in the whirlwind.
                              Try
that new way to embrace.

Fear me.
I am the man,
the hangman in the egg,
the guard in the teardrop.
                              Push me
over the edge."

DARK   RIVER

Shallows beside me,
easily water slides.
Pebbles grow no hair
where the slicing fish
dart their thither and hither;
knots of redroot
clench to a cortical node
that thinks deep mud,
original perturbation.
I wash my hands
until the fingers are numb
and the flushed skin raw.

They say there's an otter here.
I wait and watch,
remembering a blunt brown head,
a torpedo body
coining a million bubbles,
a trail of dimes
flashing and swerving illusions
of silver fortune.
The reeds have begun to shake.
The wind is rising.

The wind and the river are rising
as late light drops
the broad bar of hemlock
in black across
fast dwindling stones;
the April run-off brings
depth to every chill
and sucks dead trees

clean of their last cloyed hunger,
eats at roads.

Tread softly now.
The bank bends here. The tree
becomes a creature,
spells out guilt or love;
the hemlock leans
against the wind; it hides
rebellions of the weather
with its hands.

And here I am my loss,
in darkness dark.
Little but sound remains,
a whispering, rumpling
mimicry of syllables of love,
of mouthing sibillants.
Walk soft. The black
flints nudge at feet;
the creepers tangle thighs;
the branches knock;
there's rareness in the air.

Yet it's not altitude
that makes us breathe
in difficulty;
it is dark that's caught
the pulling lungs upon their hesitance,
and found the stillness
nudging every breath,
the presences that brood
where we contain
this colder river than the human will.

KEEP MOVING

Keep Moving!
     Somewhere, out of the dark, a voice,
a raggety shuffle, a slump of backs, a dank
sour smell of uniforms.

I can't guess what
formidable warped memory has blocked
itself out from my mind yet left the voice.
Keep Moving!
      Something lumbers in distress
through foregrounds filled with bodies. Is it food?
Fresh clothing? Papers? There's a little space
of itch upon the rough back of my hand
that cries for scratching. Something fills my nose
with — is it dust? Or smoke?
                  Move! I said Move!
I strain my ears to hear the usual joke
and muffled curse that would prove boredom ease,
but somehow someone's fallen on his knees
just at the edge of vision: is he drunk?
The head in front of me is shaven, blank,
and wobbles stupidly. We must be sick.
This memory isn't mine. The needle's stuck
in someone else's groove and won't go on.
Keep Moving There! Keep Moving!
                     Something's gone
away from thinking; some cog doesn't click
and mesh productively ; my tongue feels big:
it would be nightmare if the tired sag
of shoulders weren't a comfort, ruling out
enquiry as an effort beyond hope.

It would be nightmare, but it isn't fact
as nightmare is; it doesn't think escape
or consequence ; it simply moves, exact
in clumsiness and ignorance, a shape
too gross for comprehension.
                   I am here
a moving lump in space, in time, no more.
I keep on moving. Something tells me *Move!*
Slowly the mass is swallowed by the door.

DREAMING AND WAKING

for Kathleen Raine

Clarity shakes, dissolves.
I walk air in my dream,

stilled as a planing bird
yet moving on and on
beyond the edge of land
above the sliding sea,
steered by a breathless will,
inevitable and sure,

only to wake and stretch
my body in the bed
and know my flesh assert
its plenitude and loss.
The gross returns. It binds
the nerve, the hand, the eye.
I cannot find the dream.
The sunlight shines like lead.

But Time is only Time
and only veils. Though mist
may alter shapes and names
they spell the things we are
and point where we were born
beside this shifting sea
and guide us to our place
upon those paths of air.

AMONG THE STONES

Here we enter
upon stonescape,
hunched stones white
as the white mare
nuzzling by furze
and bulrush tattered
filmy white
by the spend of seed,
the grey outcrops
lumping up
from the birth-heaves of earth
their splayed limbs
prey to the tatter
and scab of lichen,

their skulls nudging
the stone walls
toppling to waters:
here we have pushed
to the edge of everything;
I touch
your hand, sharing
a stone harbour
depopulated
by sucking seas
and far beckonings,
exile voices
lighting like crows
on the gapped thatch
humpy with moss:
the end of the road
has brought us a place
of separations.
It grows late.
The sea ruffles
white at the land's edge;
winds wander,
wrinkling the grass;
the black curraghs
shudder their skins
on the desolate shore,
and it is late;
we have only this moment:
turn to me here, at last,
and hide
your head in the hollow
of my shoulder;
darkness is travelling
from the West
to drag our hands apart;
I watch
your mouth kiss wind
by the seaward stones,
and twilight trembles
into its haze
as birds weave crying
across the sea,
and I am stone,

the long parting
with us again
for all the years
of wandering
towards this meeting;
centuries dazzle me
in your eyes
with lost memories,
long kinship,
but we are met
among the stones
and must part again
as once
before or many
times before
in other places
other times.
Stones glimmer
as the darkness falls
and sounds of crying
fill the sea
that is our
separating tide.
We are ourselves
in being borne
apart. Our vision
is not yet.
We are the prisoners
of the stones
and this the only
place on earth
appropriate to our
mystery; this
alone is where
our spirits may
deny and welcome
their embrace,
renew again
their loss and love
upon the edge
of sea and night
between the shapes
of breath and death:

upon this edge
all motions meet
and shape the image
of a time
(who knows if it is
near or far?)
in which we share,
as once we shared,
the clarities
of all we are,
and walk together
through the stones
that stir with life
to sense us pass
and all these
separations are
no more than whispers
of the grass.

LAKESIDE INCIDENT
for Herbert Siebner

Slowly the vision grows.
A hand and then a hand
reach up through the ice,
a face, a blinded face,
mouthing, that cannot speak,
a helpless tongue that turns
around forgotten words,
a sleeve of crystal blue
lying upon the scarred
grey mirror of the cold
that can reflect no hint,
a body inching up,
a figure from a page
of quatrocento dream
suddenly obscured
by nothing but my stare.
I watch the cloak extend
slowly from nape to heel.
Upright, the man begins
to speak again. The mouth

repeats an ancient tune
I cannot understand.
The face is half my own
and half a lucid beast's,
as words, untroubled, lost
only to meaning, spin
a pattern that repeats
the patterns of the frost
upon the bracken's crisp
I brush with helpless boot.
The lake reflects the sky
and dazzles in the sun
which burns the page; a hole,
the size, first, of a coin,
grows angry at its edge;
the vellum twists and browns
into a wall of rock.
I stand before the rock.
There is no cave or door.
The sky is grey as lead.

And far below me, where
I stand upon a shelf
of breaking rock, the waters
race in brackish foam.
I beat upon the rock.
There is no answering voice.
Only a tattered rag
of blue hangs on a thorn.

TO SOMEONE FROM EXILE

I

There must be a message
to send you.
       There must be ways
of making the message,
of counting the syllables,
          shaping
the shape of the way I speak to you

when I am speaking.
There must be, surely,
a bottle to throw in the sea
and a carrying tide.

But you are my
absence;
my questions lose their tracks
in the sift of your sands,
my rain-clouds break
on mountains of elsewhere,

and
the lifted hands are the hands
of unknowing strangers.

II

If you forgive me for silence
you are forgiving
the mountain its shape
or the wind the sound of the trees;
there are notes between notes
in every music
and the face of the god
is the place of his absence,

though, God knows, I am no god
but a dust-stained traveller
tired by never taking
a step from his door,

a man with a mission
to venture upon no mission,

the loudest frog in a swamp
where there are no rains.

THE DOORS
for Cecil Collins

I understand very little
these days.

        Doors
open upon fields
from which the towers stride,
flags in their fists,
        or on
seas boiling in between
grey walls of solid mist,
a patch of red, a flag
upon some tossing scrap
that might have life,
        or on
even another door,
a face upon the door,
byzantine beggar named
saint by the bite of steel.
Myself, I open none:
they open on my sight
and close, as a machine
opens, closes, clicks
a predetermined range
of pictures to instruct
the hopeful ignorant mind;
and yet there is no means
to make connections.
        Here
steps lead up to a shrine
in which a Virgin burns
within an arch of bones,
and now the door swings shut,
and another gapes;
a crowd upon a barge
is feasting, lifting cups
of heavy gold; the mast
is garlanded with furze
lit by a setting sun;
one man is half a goat.
I lean towards the view,
mouth dry, throat taut.
        The door
clangs shut, an iron slam.
Now, at my back, a hinge
cries out, and, there, a child
sleeps in a marble lap,

tears dried upon its cheek.
Again it shuts.
        Again
I hear. I turn around,
and turn, it seems, for days,
confused, unable, held
back from each escape
by chains upon my feet;

by night I scratch my name
with nails upon the floor,
Adamus Pinxit, then
what I believe the date;
though nothing here is mine
I must record the one
pretension that remains
in words that half express
what I am now become,
a sleep through which the dreams
make unobstructed way
until one dawn the doors
hold firm, and upon one
a fist will beat, and I,
at limits of my chain,
will reach to open, sweat
to open, then, impelled
at last upon my hour,
cry *Enter,* only trust
what enters will be good,
what answers will explain.

STARDUST
for Sean Virgo

Time grows fragmentary.
Eyeball on a string
swings through the zodiac...
face in a spoon...
Gentleman's Relish
has another name

urbane in Latin,
meaning what? To whom?

We listened from hard desks.
The porcelain inkwells
held the yellow blob
of the lamp like cheese.
Dip your pen.
Mine was a blotty name.
Dying must f ace fragments
much like these,

scattered, random,
fumbling scraps together.
What, my father asked,
are all these parsons?
Where do they come from?
I read a detective novel
at his bedside,
looked at him too often,

bored, impatient, tender. Now I bore
others with a turbulence
they can't share
and I don't wish them to;
my trouble's mine.
I see Orion's arrow
sharp and near

with — is it Blake's
that bow of burning gold?
A candleflame
reflected in a spoon
makes appetite a myth.
Profound? or mad?
I think there's darkness
in the Parthenon

and darkness everywhere.
I could control,
once, every marble
in the hustling game.

Now colours roll apart.
Am I to die?
Or is it merely hard
to write my name?

THE PRISONER

Only the darkness matters,
I am in the dark,
a voice implying fingers,
head, inquiring smile,
am innocent, am guilty,
whatever you believe.

I saw the outside last
some years ago;
no-one, not even myself,
knows how many years;
all that is certain is
that my statements echo
like a stone in a well:
I drop through aeons
every time I whisper;
hear me fall !
There is no end to falling.
I live way back.

This, you say, is wrong.
Is wrong, Is Wrong
echoes round and round.
I should be new.
And *New, New* echoes;
every word is echoed,
even the clink
of tin plates on the floor.

Still, I agree.
It would be good to be able
to think in terms like *new*
to believe that *old*

meant something different from it
and to have
an individual face,
not that of the dark.

It would be good, that is,
were good a word
that echo couldn't echo.
But it echoes.

Only the darkness matters.
We are in the dark,
voices implying something,
touch implying more.
But all that matters happens
like the darkness, total,
all-conflating, echoing.

Light would blind us now.

THE FELL OF DARK
for Patrick Creagh

Hard to write of this.

The bed stirs, wells
sweat and sour wine.
The beam, a warped plank,
feathered and soft, sheds
mist; a blank sea
opens between walls.
I am out, at odds,
calling for gulls, the lost
others, damned, drowned.
Slug-grey water shifts
at my head's roll; the pillow
stinks of woman, big
body I once had,
parcels of meat lumped
together with string, garters,

suddenly human, mouth
open, a tooth black.
Hard to awake from this.

Hard to awake from this
and not lie, answer
Bad dream. Bad.
Turn over! Sleep again!
This is no dream. The thing
adrift pretends no islands
nor beneficent wind.
Lagoons are for the proud
swindlers, the easy mouths
that speak soft and hold
cambric to the plaguey
tenements of their teeth;
this is adrift on more
than fear of the dirty cuff.
It travels on itself
until it ends. I bend
my body like a hook
to hold its meat secure
until the finish bites.
Hard to rely on this.

Hard to rely on this
assured fatigue. The cramp
may come back in its hair
and heaviness. The end
may be continuance masked.
I hang on to my breath's
unbalance and my pulse.
I am awake — awake
in the most proper, least
indestructable sense;
yet still there are no gulls,
no grey-wing hurtlers cracked
crimson at the beak,
no black-capped harrowers;
the gone leave me alone.
I shall not suffer yet.

Three o'clock. I nudge
a hot dismembered leg.
There's butchery in the skull.
A monstrous lolling breast
swags on the nearmost hatch.
A finger blocks a door.
Hair crawls down to the sea,
a thick and stifling tide,
and I must look for lips.
I will not look. I turn.
The gull I thought was there
has vanished. Ropes drip sweat.

Surely this is all.
This all is all I am.
There are no farther seas.
This is the place they come,
the ghosts and mysteries meant.
Doubt hones me on a wheel
till I am sharp to cut
almost through my lids.
I very nearly see
not islands, not lagoons,
but through the looming ice
the whirlpool's wheel, believe
 the message that I bring
is what I am myself,
the message that must die
unspoken. Or unheard.

Here is another dawn.
The sea is stiffening, trapped
between this and the next.
The spirit enters waste
sargassoes of unreal
conformables and miles.
The pillow melts my head.
I flow into the day
and hear, again, the gulls.

No-one may answer this.

THE FOOL OF TIME

for Tony Connor

I

It was not that we wanted him. Business was good,
the house new, all in health; we asked no luck,
had almost forgotten the story, till my wife
turned to me, (he was shambling down the street,
his hands dithering, and his pale eyes wide),
and said, "It is a sign of grace, of grace."

She knew he would stop here. I had not known
she knew so easily what I had seen
weeks ago, that somehow we had need
of someone coming, childless as we were,
but that the someone should be yellow-haired,
slack-jawed, shambling, and should come near,
stand at the gate and smile, and I would say
the usual greeting: this we had not known.

He lived with us through time that Spring and Summer,
always a little lonely, like a bird
singing his own song, quietly at home
in his own song, yet somehow of our house.
I don't think he said anything for days,
but only ate and slept in the attic room.,
covering pieces of paper with squares and circles,
diagrams of where his mind would play
if he were quite himself, and on his walls
circles and squares in circles, up and down,
until the room was like a thing of wire
humming in the cross winds of the day,
an abstract music, not of grace or pity,
but strange and still as feathers on a stone,
alien, separate, strange. And then one day
we saw him walk away into the West.

II

I watched my own face in the bathroom mirror
watching my own face as within my mind
squares and circles, circles upon squares
shifted patterns through the emptied air.

He had been gone a day, or maybe two;
his face kept coming in between my face
and where my face looked back, until I found
my own mouth drooping sideways like his own.

I did not understand. I did not know
how in his quiet he had been so near:
thoughts of strange music twisted in my nerves.

Bewitched by silence or the luck of time,
it seemed he had not yet gone, yet I had seen him
walking, shambling, out towards the West.

III
Then things began to change. Not that the days
were any different in the common way,
but as if I were almost something else
watching the commonplace with different eyes.

I was a stone placed in the space of air.
Earth happened round me, and not where I went;
time visited me like birds, and warmth and love
rubbed themselves against my sense like cats.

Even the seasons spun upon my hub
so that the blossom of the laburnum fell
directly for my gaze, an offering rain
of yellow falling round me for my good.

I sometimes wondered then if I were dead
because I was so still, yet everywhere
life looked at me and happened at my smile
as if my living were the cause of life,

so that was not quite feasible. Besides,
my own life had its pulse and happened to me
in the old way — kindness, pain, despair,
love-longing, taste, and smell: I was alive,

but if I were alive it seemed dimensions
had been altered. Only where I was
could life be lived and seen as living to me,
being round me as I stood and smiled.

One cannot put a period to such times;
like the agelong epics of the dream
that happen in the spasm of a clock,
it may have been ten days or only seconds,

save that I know life looked at me for days.

IV
It made a difference. I had always known
obscurely how the skin had spun from seed
and seed in darkness from some other lover
who altered into fatherhood as I changed,

and I had read how, somewhere, one first Adam
stood within the centre place of earth
just as I stood; and, of course, I knew
something of ways and minds, but this was act
and not a myth or thought. I watched my hand
feeling the air move round it like a bud.

And I suppose I slept. It was in the autumn,
and how long I slept I do not know.
Winter occurred to me like phrases offered
by a stranger. Snow was given like bread.

But through this I slept surely, though I knew,
was, indeed, tremendously aware,
of everything that happened as I slept,
locked in the crystal of a square and circle

and a circle in a square, a seed
of nothingness held where the splitting spectrum
had its breath, and where light came to grow
its own shape and its colours through my sleep.

I did not think about it at that time,
thinking only about the cold and snow,
the branches that grouped black about my peace
to guard me as I stood within time's silence,

but thinking is not all. I was alone
and in my solitude was more than God,

being what God is in man, not words
and images that form what he is called,

yet was quite pitiless, felt no compassion,
only an understanding that all ways
moved on their ways about me, and that I
required no warm emotions from my selves

but something else beyond. Through me the light
came to disclose the country I had signed.

V
I had signed the country with my name,
but had not known my name. I had not known.
I did not know the signature I signed.

Was it the crystal or the words of light,
the broken colours happening in my name?
The question troubled me, then, like a fool,
time happened to me, standing at my gate.

Time happened to me like the earth. It seemed
I must make room. Some half-remembered story
made me give a usual greeting, bring
him to the attic, watch him smile and stare.

For days there were no words, just squares and circles,
circles on squares on all the walls of the room.
Then they began to change, a skein of wire
sketching all the rhythmic ways of minds

until I could not go to see him there,
being afraid to meet with my own world
fixed in someone else's walls and hands,
and could not bear the look upon his face;

until, indeed, it seemed the house would fall
because the walls were blossoming like a grave,
until I felt the silence round the house
would burst before the worlds behind the door,

and I found myself praying. Yes, I prayed.
It was not that I was so much afraid,
but that the world he had was real and true
and throbbed somehow, I don't know how it was.

And then I walked away into the West.

THE DESTINATION

This is the place: the room hacked
out of the deep of the black rock,
walls trickling, air chill,
roof invisible. Boots knock
endless echoings far back
up narrowing tunnels, the grilles locked.

Here it stands on its wet slab,
six-foot bronze of a man-bird,
bat-wing split, and claw foot
rigid, locked on the last word
gaping the tongued beak. Whitened eyes
glare as at light that blazed, charred.

Rigor has twisted the hooked hands.
Icarus? Legend deludes fact
with far history. This is here,
unnamed, unnameable, the exact
creature and cadaver, bone seared
stiff in its leaping, loin cracked.

On the walls graffiti: small heads
withered as pumice, gouged smiles,
huge breasts and members posed in acts
abstract and terrible. One girl
contains two lovers. One man
bends to a beast, his hands curled.

Nothing appals them; taking shame
into extremity, they destroy
face, feature, name. It is a cold

357

annihilation of the way
they dare not look. A huge dog
leers over a dead boy.

This is the place. We are here now,
the falling figure ruined, scarred,
the idiot crowd, in a labyrinth,
the gate we stumbled in at barred.
There is one final room ahead.
Regard the doors. Regard. Regard.

THE EDGE

Cloud below me. This is vertigo.
I am higher than a kite. My bulk
swerves on the slackening string. My canvas shivers,
flaps, blurts, flattens. Winds could tear out my side
and scatter my ribs like sticks. I soar and plunge
down, down, down. Does she guess as she takes my hand?
Her body interprets hunger. Her tongue is hot.

Clouded upon the pillows, drifting sideways,
the nerve of attachment holds firm but the window is black
and there is a night wind riding between the stars
of earth and the stars of sky. I have lost track
of all the constellations, which to keep
to the right or to the left, above or below,
and there's no tug on the string. I will her to wake.
I want to open the window. I want to breathe
in these expanding voids, breathe in, breathe out,
Icarus soaring upwards, but not to fall
as I fall now upon the bedclothes, scattering
conscience with a kiss. *I'm tired...tired...*
*No more...not just now...*There is no more now.
I am released to the air on the edge of the building,
pinned out on the stone like a bat to be finally launched
free of this Minotaur country....

                I shake her, frightened.
Love is the only place where the window is barred.

THE DOG IN THE NIGHT TIME

There is no dog.
The night's a crumpled sheet
winking and grinning
to time's jut and heave.
Here in the broken garden
my mouth is dry.

Were there folk at home
I'd have no problems —
the choked intelligible scream,
the hands
lumpy with knuckles, shaking,
the familiar
rasp of threat in my throat —
but no-one's there,
and nothing even to steal,
no locks, no dog.

And the night sweats, wrestling,
gasps hot gusts
between the moist boughs,
thickening what's to come
in clumsy terrors of release.
Grass shakes.
Dangerously, I creak open
the futile door
to flatter vacancy with caution,
roll
the wobbling ball of torchlight
along walls
that stretch then crumple it
on corners braced
against absurdity
to deaden echoes,

and am trapped, ridiculous.
The night
beyond me shudders, stiffens,
holds back till
dams can't but break;
I pause to hear it come

and in the mirror
on the landing see
the two hot eyes,
the watchful snarling fangs.

AT LOST LAKE
for Kathleen Raine

Generous with movement
time shapes whatever may be.
Beautifully the spread
ripples link and blame
their overlapping mirrors.
This is infinite sea
contrived into particular
conscience and unison.

Memory is dissolved
by memories in this
dip of the shining oar;
the serial tremors sent
towards the surrounding shore
irregularly pass
their optimum of ease
and lose astonishment

on distance far in time,
or travel fury back
in failing combat, waned
successively by strokes
that, past their origins,
presume a different tack.
I rest upon my oars
to have the stillness make

its peace with running hours.
The lake assents in glass
pre-certainty. The boat,
lodged over moving sky,
allows a cloud to hold
my dark reflected face

one second, then dissolve
its features with a sigh

into the lifting wind.
Again I dip my oars.
The mirrors overlay
each other, travelling fast
from this purpose out,
as if I were a cause
who only am a mind
whose memories, outraced

and overlaid, re-form
the hesitance of flux
to which decisions dip
their arbitrary blades,
intent upon the need
of these successive shocks
to keep direction clear
and all reflection blurred.

THE SHORE

Lanes of light lead down
to the deserted shore,
the empty standing tower.
Beside the fields of shells
the abstract dance of wind
is spinning scarves of sand
upon the patterning dunes
to phantom runes and spells.

The muted ocean lies
horizoned silver where
no boats will mesh the deep
and peopling swim of tide.
Within the tower the nets
hung salt-stiff on the wall
are sifting into sand,
the bleached door open wide.

So space before time was,
and here we find our end,
see down all lanes of light
this breath's perpetual place,
and in the tower our snares,
and in the fields of shells
our prayers, and in the sands
our dance of love or hate.

The abstract dance of wind
beside the open door,
the silvered ebb of sea,
remain as darkness folds
the visionary lanes
and we swing in the tide,
each knotted current loud,
each sea-deep dark and old.

ACROSS THIS DISTANCE,
IN CODE, IN PLAIN

Lovers together
use words
that have no meaning
save in their
distinct country
where light breaks
open in laughter
and thought dies.

So, although we are not
those lovers,
yet both lovers
in others arms,
I make private
what should be private,
flaunting the riddle
to watching walls,

and ask you now,
Do you remember

the pink flowers
nodding on rock
at the tide's edge,
and the bulrushes
shrouded in tatters
of wisped seed?

Do you remember
the old woman
mumbling with ropes
of tow for hair,
mouth toothless,
eyes leaking,
stumbling among
the polished cars?

And do you remember
behind the carved
and runic slab
on the great wall
the piercing sweetness
of small birds,
the blind darkness,
the shreds of straw?

Remembering these
myself, finding
them side by side
as if words
of an old language
marching syntax
towards a ceremony
for love,

I place them thus
for you, knowing
flower and seed-time,
age, death, birth
finally simple
as the pebble
upon the shore
that I picked
and gave you.

Index of First Lines

A bad day; the kids jabbing   (1962)   251
Achievement?   1974   293
A drunk poet in a woman's bed   (1968)   154
After the first two miles there is only a body   1968   31
After the struggle   (1961)   69
All the swans are asleep, and I remember   (1960)   186
All winter I   (1972)   278
A long white room as cobwebbed as the sea;   1960   28
A mountain wrinkled   1971   57
An alley of old statues   (1969)   318
And down they clack. Four pairs of hands   (1959)   123
An old man picking plums   (1967)   42
April remainders me upon this green   (1967)   246
A Saint, they said, *A Saint!*   (1968)   175
A single rock,   (1970)   310
As I remember it, the place was old;   1962   34
A slice of lemon in my tea,   (1962)   244
Astonishment commands   1972   110
A sword thrust into stone   (1970)   308
As you came naked   (1974)   102
At forty sensual enough, no grey   (1965)   293
At forty we are restless. I peel dry skin   (1965)   298
"At last I have self-destruction.   (1964)   336
At last the animals   (1969)   179
At sixty four in the family swing   (1970)   130
At the end of the avenue, the house   (1954)   34
At thirteen older than I   (1962)   78

Backside strapped   1969   187
Below the round and roof-swerve of the chapel   (1956)   89
Be with me, Muse. I need the dream   (1976)   100
Black-laced, black beaded, delicate, this creature   (1968)   172
Bound together   1972   220

"Call me ancient.   (1964)   334
Casement returns. Already stories   (1966)   197
Clarity shakes, dissolves.   1974   339
Climbing up from the boat, he must have figured   (1960)   68
Cloud below me. This is vertigo.   1971   358
Coloured the incredible flame   1962   294

Construct a moor, a valley, and a sea.   1960   85
Constructing my poem   1969   191

Darkness, comfortable with strangeness,   1968   117
Darkness remembers...   1972   106
Death is Webster's territory. It helps   (1968)   66
Dirty snow at the base   (1963)   74
Drogheda grey in a grey wind,   (1966)   196
Drunk above North Dakota, stoned out of my mind,   (1967) 243

Everything happens again.   (1963)   50
Every three seconds some child dies of hunger   (1966)   138
Every time your name   (1967)   271
Every travelling is of the soul   (1970)   307
Everywhere it happens.   1972   109
Explain this! I am ordered.   1973   272

Faces invent the past.   (1969)   322
Far off in the night a drum   (1976)   238
Find a sea shell on the shore;   (1947)   115
First Light: the mouth begins   (1967)   302
Flesh bulges as she drags her corset down,   1962   150
Forbidden drink,the arms of women   (1966)   198
Forgive me,   1972   215
Forgive me that I make of love   (1961)   137
For rehabilitation   (1963)   52
From a sour garden wrinkled with trees   (1958)   292

Generous with movement, time   (1967)   360
Girl at a bright lit window: 1971   59
Girl to feathers over the death-spumed sea: 1958   135
Girls in black leather touch his heart   (1959)   124
Grading his paper, I see him standing   (1967)   247

Half asleep,tonight I recall the poems.   1971   234
Halfway to where God only knows,   (1960)   283
Hand moving where your   (1975)   155
Hands twining grasses   1968   149
Hard to write of this.   (1970)   350
Having built the maze of words, stones, trees,   1960   131
Hawking and spitting at the bar of the dead,   1964   201
He answered pools with pebbles; where the sun   1960   130
He has set spies upon your door;   (1962)   263

He must be he   1977   216
Here is the place humanity was made —   1962   137
Here is the track, between rocks   (1960)   295
Here the dawn is slow.   (1964)   333
Here we enter   (1967)   340
Her leather coat   1977   277
He thought of buying this old house,   (1960)   120
His car was found abandoned near the bridge.   (1967)   233
Histories walk tonight;   (1966)   296

I am a monster.   (1963)   250
I am a mouth,   (1969)   171
"I am destruction   (1964)   335
I am supported in my conviction   1974   282
"I am what you suppose.   (1964)   334
I cannot quite remember   (1965)   215
I can't believe it —   1972   219
I do not know   1977   104
I do not wish   (1960)   213
I enter the tomb and remember   1958   315
If I say   1977   210
If my love were in my arms   1972   213
I have a name for it.   1968   169
I have been there: 1968   58
I have not been where you are going.   1962   313
I have remembered   (1975)   262
I journey backwards.   1968   290
I missed three trains at least   (1976)   159
I'm never certain what the message is   1960   46
In a shop advertised as selling "Aids   (1961)   103
In the rank orchard of a house   1962   29
In the station at Madras, he said *I am a Christian.*   1964   52
In the wee small hours of the morning   1971   230
In Venice once, a girl —   1972   109
'I sometimes think that stone,' he said,   1958   87
I stamp on the ice of a man a hundred years dead.   (1963)   236
I take up my pen... (pauses,scratches,   (1966)   198
I talk of *Amours de Voyage.* You shake your head,   (1969)   317
Item, skull. A clutter of dry bones.   (1966)   190
It is not enough to be wise;   (1969)   89
It is over, you tell me.   1972   214
It looks, she says, *so silly,*   1972   214
I took off my suit   (1971)   276

367

It's not too much to say   1972 275
I touch your nipples with my tongue   (1977) 162
It was not that we wanted him. Business was good   (1958) 353
It was on a summer's evening.   1969 201
It was six foot four of my father   1962 40
I understand very little   (1970) 345
I walked into the mountain heart.   1958 129
I walk my reappearance   (1963) 76
I was born in the year   (1962) 232
I wear bone   (1968) 173
'I will not let you go'. Our fears   (1966) 208
I will not sleep   (1963) 218
I would send you   1972 210
I write this   (1970) 229

John Arthur walks the tideline-scribbled sand,   1960 38

Keep Moving!   1968 338
'Kiss me, and if that is old hat   1960 151

Lanes of light lead down   1958 361
Language, a peeling fence, cracks at the lean   1958 226
Laughter we had   (1972) 156
Learning   (1967) 225
Let in the clear,   (1972) 222
Let us, in this pagan Spring   (1960) 154
Listen. How long have you listened?   1960 94
Listen. This is   1974 20
Lost in the ordinary street, he turned   1960 127
Love in a cotton dress.   1958 90
Love is eternal but not   1972 108
Lover, have you learned to hear,   1973 148
Lovers together   (1967) 362

Memory moves through the figments   1972 112
Mercy, Pity, Peace, and Love.   1960 118
Moon-tusked, wrenching at roots,   (1968) 165
Mother of myths, the old wonder,   (1966) 195
Music he asked of that grave general,   1955 131
My land had no customs. Habits, tricks   (1960) 36
My language thickening, I end the class,   1971 227

Names are no matter. Bony-kneed,   (1961) 206

Ninth month ending, (1967)	301
No longer do we expect (1971)	140
No, she said 1977	220
Nothing of beauty, 1962	143
No two men equally admit 1977	216
Off Massawa (1963)	54
Old enough to be 1972	211
Once I knew a pond 1971	165
Once in the cave it was black as your hat. 1960	91
Once more, once more (1975)	159
One word from her (1974)	101
Only the darkness matters, 1974	349
Only to tell you why these structures are 1960	228
Our fathers were both Artillerymen, (1964)	60
Our trades being one, across the sea (1960)	39
Out of my childhood birds (1959)	164
Part of the need 1972	107
Peter was nearly a rock: 1971	63
Poems should be wisdom 1974	325
Proud and ashamed (1975)	157
Rathmines clocktower as near (1961)	204
Rattle and jolt of the cart 1962	44
Reading these words 1972	216
Recalling it is enough (1976)	160
Red curtains move (1965)	253
Remove your sleeping mask 1968	237
Runnelled and fanged (1969)	323
Seated on well-lip (1969)	177
Seated, suddenly shamed (1975)	157
Seeing her in Her various disguises, (1961)	104
Sergeant Casey called them fucking niggers. 1971	65
Seventeenth of November, Nineteen Sixty: (1967)	332
Shallows beside me, (1972)	337
She rinsed her mouth. (1971)	272
She, unrehearsed in the play, meets 1960	147
Silence, Exile, Cunning. A sham boast, 1969	199
Since it becomes us 1977	217
Since love (1972)	211
Sleep's grown a killer; 1968	299

Slowly the vision grows   1974   343
Smell the nice scent, she said. The table slithered   1974   27
So cold, so cold?   1972   264
So far, so good. I daren't commit myself   (1958)   287
Something is changing.   (1967)   303
Steering the weeks towards that sudden   (1969)   306
Straddled the walls, then ran like lemurs   1962   41
Strain the cord round, tight as breeches   1955   29
Stranger than fiction   (1973)   209
Sudden as a mirror, the red house   1960   25
Suddenly, light!   1972   107
Suppose the moon,   1972   217
Surely it is about to happen again.   1968   114

Tall girl, tall boots,   (1969)   175
Tame jackdaw on his head, my father   1962   25
Taste! you said.   1977   264
Tattered by light   (1949)   289
That crazy hat   (1973)   209
That day the barren island swooped like a gull   1955   132
The attitudes of flowers and trees are strange   1958   226
The big hands idle on the robe-smooth stone,   1958   136
The blue coat hangs   (1957)   88
The blue day was an apple in the hand   1958   135
The cat stood under the lilac.   1958   174
The cliff crumbles;   1972   219
The crumpled villages, guide-booked and mapped,   1960   224
The dead girl   (1963)   243
The ditch in Hunber Lane   (1962)   26
The earth is   1971   166
The first film that I saw   1969   189
'The first time's never good   1971   274
The girl was young. He whispered to his mate   (1959)   121
The inventor of   1971   48
The last time I drank here   (1963)   81
The man in the corner with the nervous tic   (1959)   121
The market shudders canvas;   (1969)   328
The peacock cries.   1974   188
The place she sleeps I know   1977   212
The pretence of music to have something to say   (1958)   142
The primrose watches me   (1971)   161
There is no dog.   1968   359
There must be a message   1971   344

The road was black that Easter night; 1969	91
These are the people of exodus. 1960	84
The sliding planes of stone, the stacked	33
The stones were round where he picked them, (1950)	133
The street is done in greys and browns; 1955	114
The whole of this (1972)	208
The wind's in the west tonight, (1964)	254
They called her 'Angel', sardonic 1962	30
They kiss, fumble. (1969)	178
This for Johnnie Question 1960	125
This happiness... 1972	221
This infant staggerer carries round 1962	286
This is dangerous. 1972	111
This is our land. (1968)	170
This is the place: the room hacked (1967)	357
This poem for her 1972	104
This poem is to a person 1971	265
This rain-wet chick (1959)	144
This worn-out word, (1962)	224
This year's beginning, a dead age (1953)	116
Though we are loyal 1977	262
Though writhing nightly 1977	265
Time grows fragmentary. 1971	347
To claim her love (1967)	146
Today you caused and knew you caused (1960)	161
To fall in love with Ireland 1969	182
To hold on stone, exactly, (1969)	327
Tom, Tom, brass in a woodwind landscape, 1955	133
Tomorrow I may hear. 1972	273
Tonight's my birth-night. I can't sleep. One leg (1972)	286
Too cautious to say (1958)	218
Trapped by grief, we (1963)	80
Travelling east (1964)	329
"Trust me. (1964)	336
Turning again 1977	221
Twelve years ago. (1963)	72
Under a Kerry hedge, light shaking (1966)	197
Under our window 1972	212
Under the rock is an iron ball. (1956)	84
Vertigo is my territory, Man (1968)	164

Waistcoat wrinkled brown as puddles, 1962	45
Wearing an old oat in the sweat of sun, 1960	145
We call it Memory. (1967)	65
We huddled under the stairs among wet raincoats (1965)	55
We lived ramshackle that summer in a cabin 1971	248
We melted down remnants of armies in the tin cup 1958	36
Westfield Lane, a green switchback 1962	32
What could be less heroic? Rusted nails (1961)	205
What was seed, was fish, (1974)	290
Whenever your name (1967)	215
When I began 1974	24
When in the hot night (1968)	147
When you can say *Long Ago* of your own memories 1971	282
Whether the quiet breaks us, or we the quiet, 1960	43
Who will read this? Many of them are dead. (1963)	49
Wine-drunk and love-drunk both (1970)	156
Wovoka believed (1963)	252
Wrestle, Jacob, with the stone angel, (1958)	96
Writing this naked, 1972	279
Year by slow year I 1974	24
Yes, she is sure. It's two weeks late (1959)	122
You entered upon the company (1972)	101
You have a good seat, bright-saddled 1962	320
You'll need a guide. This Baedecker of the back (1961)	128
You, Who exist 1969	100

Biography

Poet, anthologist, editor, teacher, biographer, art and literary critic, historical writer, initiated witch and occultist, Robin Skelton has pursued, and gained, a considerable reputation in many artistic and philosophic fields.

He came to Canada in 1963, already the author of five collections of poetry and the author or compiler of nine other books. He taught at the University of Victoria from 1963 until 1992 when he retired. During that time, he taught in the Department of English and then in the Department of Creative Writing of which he was the founding Chairman in 1973. In 1967, together with John Peter, he founded *The Malahat Review* and was the sole editor for a time.

He has had approximately 100 books published and is working on several new projects. He is presently a co-operator of Reference West, publishers of the award-winning Hawthorne Series of chapbooks. He lives in Victoria, B.C. with his wife.